Praise for
The SAIC Solution

At SAIC, Dr. Beyster led a talented team of scientists and engineers in addressing some of the country's most complex and challenging technical problems in support of national defense. These are truly amazing accomplishments, and anyone who knows the history knows that Dr. Beyster's ideas, vision, and personal example were central to SAIC's success. Many have tried to imitate his style and organizational strategy, but no one has succeeded with such magnitude.

—Dr. Anthony J. Tether
Director, Defense Advanced Research Projects Agency (DARPA)

It's not often when a brilliant scientist is also a brilliant entrepreneur. It's even less common for this same person to have the unique skills needed to take the business they founded and preside over its continued growth for an extended period of time. Dr. Beyster is one of these rare individuals, and the company he founded and grew—SAIC—is a living testament to the validity of his sometimes counterintuitive approach to business.

—Richard C. Atkinson
President Emeritus, University of California

The SAIC Solution is an inside look into the growth and dynamic culture of America's largest employee-owned research and engineering firm. Dr. J. Robert Beyster chronicles how his "people first" culture allowed SAIC to leverage its intellectual capital and stimulate transformative research with an empowered and elite team of scientists and engineers. *The SAIC Solution* is a valuable resource for prospective entrepreneurs and business leaders interested in learning the benefits of decentralized decision-making and employee ownership.

—Carl J. Schramm
President, Ewing Marion Kauffman Foundation

A fascinating account of how an outstanding nuclear physicist left a promising career as a scientist to form a unique multibillion dollar employee-owned company. Should be required reading for any potential entrepreneur contemplating a new approach to forming any successful enterprise.

—Harold M. Agnew
President, General Atomics
Director, Los Alamos Scientific Laboratory

The SAIC Solution is a rare and fascinating study of an employee-owned enterprise, enormously innovative, enormously successful. Once again a lesson in the power of a shared vision, the power of innovation, the power of inclusion, and the power of leadership.

—Frances Hesselbein
Chairman, Leader to Leader Institute

THE
SAIC
SOLUTION

How We Built an

$8 Billion Employee-Owned

Technology Company

Dr. J. Robert Beyster *with*
Peter Economy

John Wiley & Sons, Inc.

Published by John Wiley & Sons, Inc., Hoboken, New Jersey.
Published simultaneously in Canada.

Wiley Bicentennial Logo: Richard J. Pacifico

For general information on our other products and services or for technical support, please contact our Customer Care Department within the United States at (800) 762-2974, outside the United States at (317) 572-3993 or fax (317) 572-4002.

Wiley also publishes its books in a variety of electronic formats. Some content that appears in print may not be available in electronic formats. For more information about Wiley products, visit our Web site at www.wiley.com.

Except as noted, photographs used in the book appear through courtesy of SAIC.

Library of Congress Cataloging-in-Publication Data:

Beyster, J. Robert
  The SAIC solution : how we built an $8 billion employee-owned technology company / J. Robert Beyster with Peter Economy.
     p. cm.
  Includes bibliographical references.
  ISBN 978-0-470-09752-6 (cloth)
    1. High technology industries—Management. 2. High technology industries—United States. 3. Employee ownership—United States. 4. Science Applications International Corporation. 5. Engineering firms—United States—History. I. Economy, Peter. II. Title.
HD62.37.B49 2007
658—dc22
                                                                                    2006037900

10 9 8 7 6 5 4 3 2 1

*To my wife, Betty, and
my three kids: Jim, Mark, and Mary Ann,
to the hard-working and devoted employee-owners of
SAIC, and to all future employee-owners,
and those who create opportunities for
employees to become owners.*

Contents

CONTENTS

Foreword

The great promise of the American economy, especially the high-tech economy, is its seemingly inexhaustible supply of ingenuity, creativity, and breakthrough advances—innovations in computing, communications, software, and the life sciences that shape how we live, work, inform, and entertain ourselves. This country's entrepreneurial spirit and our culture of technology-driven progress continue to be—rightly—the envy of much of the rest of the world.

But there is a specter haunting America's economic miracle, the specter of a disconnect between those who help invent, market, and produce our dazzling innovations and those who benefit most from the economic value unleashed by those innovations. It's hard to explain—and, it seems, hard to reverse—but as the U.S. economy creates more and more income and wealth, that income and wealth is distributed into fewer and fewer hands.

All the data point in the same direction. The average CEO in the United States is now paid more than 400 times the salary of the average employee. The typical big company distributes 75 percent of its stock options to only its top five executives. All told, the top one percent of Americans receives 16 percent of total income—up from 8 percent just 25 years ago. As a country and a business culture, we have gotten strangely comfortable with a rising tide of inequality.

But does anyone believe that this level of inequality is desirable, sustainable, or remotely good for business? Indeed, the biggest threat to our long-term prosperity isn't the budget deficit, the trade deficit, or the status of the dollar. It's the winner-take-all ethos that has corrupted so many leaders in the executive suite and shredded the bonds between companies and the front-line employees who make those companies work.

All of which explains why the work and legacy of Dr. J. Robert Beyster and his colleagues at Science Applications International Corporation

(SAIC) are such powerful symbols of American business at its best—and why his book deserves as wide an audience as possible. At one level, Dr. Beyster's track record as an entrepreneur since 1969 illustrates the power of developing and embracing disruptive technologies. From homeland security to energy and from the environment to the life sciences, SAIC has been on the cutting edge of every field in which it operates.

But the deeper lesson behind the growth and prosperity of SAIC is the power of a distinctive and disruptive point of view—a point of view about how to build a great and enduring company, about the conditions under which talented people do their best work, and about how to combine the power of innovation with a deeply held sense of fair play. I've always believed that the best companies don't just invent and sell competitive products and services. They stand for important ideas—ideas that shape the future of an industry, ideas that reshape the sense of what's possible among customers, employees, and investors. I believe that the ideas in this book have the potential to get American business back on track, to help leaders create organizations that win big in the marketplace by building workplaces that give everyone a piece of the action.

As you read this honest, open, and instructive book, be sure to pay close attention to the twelve defining principles and the wide range of day-to-day practices that make SAIC such an incredible success story. Use a highlighter, jot down notes, and focus on the "small stuff" that Dr. Beyster shares so generously. At the same time, don't lose sight of the big picture that SAIC represents. Be sure to read the book in the context of the conventional wisdom about business in America—and appreciate what a provocative and inspiring challenge to conventional wisdom it sets out.

For example, the book offers a powerful message about the new logic of strategy, and the iron-clad connection between the values you exude as an organization and the economic value you create in the marketplace. In an era of hypercompetition and nonstop innovation, the only way to stand out from the crowd is to stand for something unique. Behind every great company I've gotten to know is a distinctive and disruptive sense of purpose—a value system—and the companies with the clearest sense of purpose are the ones that win. There's no denying the power and originality of the value system around which Dr. Beyster built SAIC.

The book also offers a welcome message about the real meaning of success. As a business leader, Dr. Beyster has always played to win, and he has enjoyed the rewards of his victories in the marketplace. But he never schemed to keep all the rewards for himself, and he was never prepared to succeed at the expense of his colleagues. He has always believed that the best way to create vast economic value is to share it widely with all who played a role in its creation. Forget the winner-take-all economy. In Dr. Beyster's world, nobody wins unless everyone who contributed to the success of the organization wins.

Finally, the book offers a mind-shifting message about the new logic of leadership. Much of our business culture is infatuated with power—amassing it, holding on to it, using it to vanquish competitors and dominate markets. In contrast, much of Dr. Beyster's leadership philosophy is about spreading freedom. And freedom, it turns out, packs a bigger wallop than power. Power is about what you can control; freedom is about what you can unleash. As this book makes abundantly clear, Dr. Beyster has not been interested in controlling his colleagues' aspirations. He has been determined to *unleash* his colleagues, to give them permission to pursue their passions, talents, and ideas—and to revel in the thrill of what they create.

All of this explains why Dr. Beyster, for all the years he ran SAIC, displayed behind his desk a poster given to him by his wife Betty. "None of us is as smart as all of us," the poster declared—a perfect mantra for the organization he built. It's no longer the job of the founder or the CEO to be the smartest person in the room. It's the job of the leader to attract the smartest thinking from the most people. As a leader, he was smart enough to recognize that he doesn't—and didn't need to—have all the answers.

For more than 30 years at SAIC, Robert Beyster succeeded bigger than most of us do because he thought bigger than most of us do. The great Michelangelo once warned: "The greater danger for most of us lies not in setting our aim too high and falling short; but in setting our aim too low, and achieving our mark."

This book shows what happens when you aim high and achieve your mark. Here's hoping that more of us will dare to aim as high as J. Robert Beyster.

WILLIAM C. TAYLOR

William C. Taylor is the founding editor of *Fast Company* and co-author of *Mavericks at Work: Why the Most Original Minds in Business Win* (New York: William Morrow, 2006).

Preface

When I founded Science Applications International Corporation (SAIC) in 1969, I had no idea that this company that has been so much a part of my life over the past 38 years would grow from one small, government contract into an $8 billion technology business powerhouse. But it has, and for that I am very pleased and grateful. For this unexpected entrepreneur, SAIC has been the ride of a lifetime.

Although many people have been touched by SAIC at one time or another in their lives, most people have not heard about the company, much less understand what it does. I attempt to rectify that situation with this book. The company has certainly not gone unnoticed where it counts—in the minds of its customers, suppliers, employees, or in the business press. SAIC is the country's largest employee-owned research and engineering company and it has often landed on *Fortune* magazine's top-10 list of America's Most Admired Companies: Computer and Data Services.

I know that some readers of this book will ask why I wrote this book and, particularly, why did I write this book *now?*

The answer is that I have watched with concern the steady erosion of America's primacy in science, engineering, and technology innovation. In 2004, the National Science Board warned that there is a troubling decline in the number of U.S. citizens who are trained to become scientists and engineers. As the Board goes on to note, this trend "threaten[s] the economic welfare and security of our country."[1] More recently, I have read numerous articles describing the decline of U.S. competitiveness in the global marketplace. This trend should worry us all.

I hope this book inspires those entrepreneurs who have considered starting their own science, engineering, or technology firms to make the leap—to turn their dreams into reality—and to encourage America's youth to join them on their journey. Our nation needs them more than ever, and the rewards are limited only by their own imagination and aspirations.

I am also concerned that many innovative firms shy away from working with the federal government. The SAIC success story clearly illustrates that doing work for and with the government can not only be good business, but it can be a deeply patriotic act. We can help to defend our shores, make our cities safer, provide our citizens with financial security and prosperity, and—in the words of the Preamble of our Constitution—"secure the blessings of liberty to ourselves and our posterity." I am extremely proud of the work we have done for our country—SAIC employees have done their part to keep federal, state, and local government agencies at the forefront of technological innovation—and I strongly encourage more companies to step up to the plate by offering their competencies to both the public and private sectors.

Finally, I sense that the time is now right to tell my SAIC story, to describe how—with the help of thousands of talented and motivated employee-owners—we built this very successful enterprise. I couldn't have written this book a decade or even a few years ago—I was too close to the company's daily operations to have either the time or the inclination to reflect on what we had done. With my retirement from SAIC in 2004, I have had time to disengage from the day-to-day operations and consider what things worked—and what things didn't. In this book, you'll find plenty of both, and you'll understand how the lessons I learned—often by trial and error—can help you grow your own business and ensure its success.

We succeeded in a very competitive industry because we had a knack for hiring extremely talented people, providing them with the freedom to create the kind of business they would be excited to work in, and giving them ownership in the business commensurate with their contributions to its success. We built SAIC on the premise that every SAIC employee counts and—no matter how big we were—that everyone could and did make a difference.

I was a demanding CEO. I gave my managers as much authority and autonomy as they wanted and could handle, but I also expected results, and I constantly monitored performance metrics and kept my finger on the pulse of *every* part of the organization, no matter how small or how far flung it might be. My job was to be the catalyst that energized the organization—to set the bar high, to keep people on their toes, to model (and insist on) the highest ethical standards, and to hold people to their promises.

Whatever kind of company you lead or work for, remember that it's mostly about people—and not so much the organization. Your organization should be designed to serve your customers, your employees, and your shareholders—they are the reason for your business. In these days of ever-increasing legislative controls over management, it is particularly important for leaders to guard against creeping bureaucracy and to ensure that their organizations are nimble and responsive to fast-changing markets, and that they are able to keep up with even faster-changing technology.

This book has been a collaborative effort, utilizing input and suggestions of many SAIC employees, both past and present. It's no accident that a particular poster—given to me by my wife, Betty—hung over my desk throughout my tenure at the helm of SAIC. This poster reads, "None of us is as smart as all of us." For me, those words ring just as true today as they did when I founded the company more than three decades ago.

I began my transition out of SAIC's day-to-day operations in late 2003. This book is focused on the company as it was up until the end of 2003. I do not currently have knowledge of the company's operations, or its future plans and initiatives beyond what is publicly available in the news media and through the company's web site. Nonetheless, the reader should be aware of the fact that SAIC became a public company on October 13, 2006. Though it was never in my mind to take that step, I wish the company and its employees well in the Wall Street world.

In the chapters that follow, I describe how our unconventional and sometimes counterintuitive approach to business was instrumental in creating a unique company with an organizational culture unlike any other. As of this writing, more than 150,000 men and women have worked for SAIC since we began our experiment more than three decades ago. It has been a very real honor and pleasure to personally meet and work with many of these employees, and together to build a company that has touched and changed the lives of people around the world. I thank them for joining and unfailingly supporting me as CEO in this adventure.

DR. J. ROBERT BEYSTER
La Jolla, California

Acknowledgments

Writing this book was not an easy task, and it proved once again that none of us are as smart as all of us. I am deeply indebted to the many people who contributed to this book—through personal interviews, e-mails, phone calls, posts to my blog, reviewing our proposal, serving on the manuscript Red Team, and a variety of other channels. There are almost too many people to thank in the small amount of space allotted to this part of the book, but I will do my best. If I have forgotten to name you, I hope you will forgive me.

I would like to thank Jordan Becker, David Binns, Joseph Blasi, Al Buckles, Ralph Callaway, Robert Craig, Tom Darcy, Tom Dillon, Steve Fisher, Roger Garrett, Karen Garson, John Glancy, Sydell Gold, Ted Gold, Eric Hazard, Michael Higgins, Mark Hughes, Neil Hutchinson, Jim Idell, Bobby Inman, Clint Kelly, Mark Kerrigan, Cheryl Louie, Nancy Anderson McLaughlin, Lloyd Mosemann, Vic Orphan, Peter Pavlics, Dave Poehlman, Gene Ray, Steve Rizzi, Steve Rockwood, Jim Russell, Barbara Schmidt, Bill Scott, Doug Scott, Dick Shearer, Ray Smilor, Martin Staubus, Peter Stocks, Charlie Stringfellow, Gael Tarleton, Matt Tobriner, Dick Wallner, Kevin Winstead, Dan Whitaker, and Ron Zollars. Thanks also to John Tishler and Kevin Goering of Sheppard Mullin. And I would like to thank SAIC for all their help and cooperation in providing photos and historical materials for the book, allowing access to employees, and reviewing the manuscript for accuracy.

Many current and former SAIC employees rose to the occasion by posting their opinions on my blog (www.beyster.com), and sending e-mail messages and letters of encouragement along the way. Their contributions were invaluable. I wish to thank the blog team of Geoff Young, Rick Dean, and Ron Arnold.

I would be remiss if I did not recognize the efforts of my front-line assistants who tirelessly supported my efforts from the beginning of SAI through my retirement—and beyond—including Helen Napoli, Barbara Schmidt, Ann Zvanovec, Ron Zollars, and Ralph Callaway. In addition, there are thousands of men and women—the employee-owners of SAIC—who deserve to be acknowledged for all they have done for me, for SAIC, and for our customers. We couldn't have done it without you, and I thank you all.

And last but not least, I would like to thank my daughter Mary Ann Beyster for convincing me that this book was something important for me to do, and then for putting the pieces in place to make it happen.

Dr. Bob Beyster, SAIC Founder, Former Chairman and Chief Executive Officer.

(Photo credit: Photograph by Eric Millette. All Rights Reserved. Reprinted with permission from photographer.)

In 1998, SAIC's employees being photographed for the cover of Forbes.

(Photo credit: Photograph by Eric Millette. All Rights Reserved. Reprinted with permission from photographer and *Forbes*.)

SAI's first office in La Jolla, California, came cheap—$2.40 per square foot per year—not bad for an office with an ocean view.

In 1969, Betty Beyster gave her husband Bob this poster for his new office.
(Courtesy of Bob and Betty Beyster.)

SAIC's portable, combat-rugged communications work stations have served the needs of all U.S. military services.

Dr. Beyster and Gene Haddad at the GA LINAC.

SAIC quickly began using skill gained from national security work to undertake projects for the nuclear energy industry. Pictured are Glen Reynolds, shown on the left, and Larry Kull.

In 1988, SAIC moved its corporate headquarters to Campus Point in San Diego, constructing seven buildings there.

When Stars and Stripes won back the America's cup from Australia in 1987, it was more than a sailing victory. It was also a technology victory for SAIC.

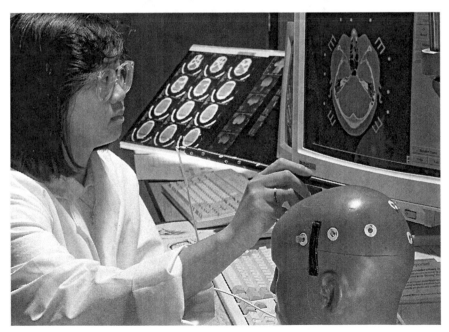

Neurosurgeons can now see the locations of their surgical instruments thanks to a system developed with SAIC expertise.

SAIC provides support to two of NASA's most important efforts—operating the Space Shuttle and building the International Space Station.

SAIC's Washington, DC, Headquarters.

SAIC divers help prepare a submarine to run underwater noise trials.

SAIC's Vehicle and Cargo Inspection Systems (VACIS) are gamma ray-based systems.

SAIC has developed a simulation capability to insert dismounted infantry into synthetic virtual environments.

The Defense Advanced Research Projects Agency's (DARPA) Grand Challenge race through the Mojave Desert was a field test of future battlefield robotic vehicle technology. Carnegie-Mellon University/SAIC's autonomous vehicles navigated to finish second and third, from an original field of 40 autonomous vehicles.

1

The Result:
An $8 Billion
Business Success

Those who contribute to the company should own it, and ownership should be commensurate with a person's contribution and performance as much as feasible.[1]

—J. Robert Beyster

Perhaps you've already been introduced to Science Applications International Corporation, or SAIC. Maybe you're one of the tens of thousands of people who have worked for the company since I founded it in 1969, or perhaps you're working on one of the company's 9,000+ current contracts. Or you might be one of SAIC's current or former customers in the public or private sector, a list that includes a veritable Who's Who of federal government leaders and agencies (like the Department of Defense, the Federal Aviation Administration, the Department of Energy, NASA, the Department of Homeland Security, and many more); a variety of state and local governments; commercial firms such as Southern California Edison, Entergy, Pfizer, and other Fortune 100 companies; and international customers such as British Petroleum, the Saudi Royal Naval Forces, and Scottish Power.

Or you might even be one of SAIC's new shareholders. This company—employee owned since the very beginning—recently completed an initial public offering in October 2006, raising $1.13 billion.

But even if you're not familiar with SAIC and its remarkable story, you've surely felt its impact on your own life. If you've ever wondered how elusive terrorists are tracked down and captured by sifting through mountains of electronic data gathered by the nation's intelligence services, you may have encountered just one example of SAIC's vast array of leading-edge database technologies. If someone you know has faced the challenge of beating cancer or AIDS, SAIC has been active in the search for cures in its role as Operations and Technical Support Contractor for the National Cancer Institute's Frederick Cancer Research and Development Center. Or, if you surfed to a web site, the pathways your computer followed from your desktop to its ultimate destination were paved by one of SAIC's former subsidiaries, Network Solutions, Inc.

Some say that SAIC is the best company that most people have never heard of. On one hand, much of SAIC's mainline work has been on federal contracts—many of which involved classified programs that are intentionally kept out of the public eye. But on the other hand, SAIC is an incredibly eclectic company—a decentralized organization that explicitly encourages and rewards entrepreneurial upstarts and initiatives in new project areas and with new customers—and it has touched the everyday lives of many people in the United States and beyond, often in unexpected ways.

SAIC's environment is one where creativity, innovation, and entrepreneurship are more than management buzzwords—they are the company's core principles. Over the past 38 years, SAIC has managed and performed on tens of thousands of contracts and it has a hard-earned reputation for succeeding on the "tough" jobs—the very complex technical and important problems few companies are willing or able to tackle. Instead of focusing on only a handful of large customers working on a small number of large contracts, SAIC historically has taken a different tack, also engaging in thousands of relatively small-dollar jobs—representing an incredibly diverse array of different projects and customers across many market sectors.

This symbiotic mix of government and commercial business might be viewed by some observers as a vice, because of the challenge of focusing on so many different kinds of businesses with so many different customers. However, SAIC's diversity of customers and contracts was a virtue and not a vice, and it was a way of life for our employees. More importantly, it was a key defensive mechanism for protecting the company from market and environmental changes beyond our control.

So, how did SAIC become the 800-pound stealth giant of American science, engineering, and technology businesses? It all began with a simple set of organizing principles (formalized a decade after being founded) that served the company well as it grew from a handful of employees in the Southern California seaside village of La Jolla, to more than 43,000 people in more than 150 locations around the world.

A SIMPLE IDEA, WELL EXECUTED

At one time, years ago, I might have been voted by my coworkers as someone "least likely to start up his own business." A nuclear physicist by trade, I was first and foremost a scientist, not an entrepreneur. I decided, however, to leave behind my comfortable career as chairman of the Accelerator Physics Department at San Diego-based General Atomic (GA) to start my own company. Before there was an SAIC, there was just SAI, which stood for Science Applications Incorporated. Only later—when we incorporated in Delaware—did the name become SAIC. We found it necessary to change the name because of the proliferation of the SAI label. Today there are many companies and other organizations that use the SAI initials, including Social Accountability International, Software Architects, Inc., and others.

SAIC was an unexpected happening. There was no grandiose plan for its future. It was just supposed to be a good place where I could work and maybe a few people could join me, so I could continue to live in San Diego and keep my wife happy.

From the beginning, SAIC was an employee-owned firm. In previous jobs with a national laboratory and then at a large corporation, I saw many people leave, taking ideas generated there to start their own companies. These entrepreneurs were quite interested in starting a company for financial rewards based on a new idea or product they had developed. They planned to start a company, grow it, and then sell it or take it public, and go on to the next business venture. That was hardly the optimal environment for research people, and it was not my intention in founding SAIC.

Our goal was to grow a company that would be stable—where the staff stayed with the company, even in hard times. In this company, creative research would be considered important, regardless of the size of the contract. Rewards would be fair. Everyone would share in the ownership of the company based on their contributions to our success. That only seemed right, especially if we expected people to work long and hard to help build the company. Also, everyone would contribute to decisions affecting the company—profit would not be the main driver. We wanted to make enough money to run the business, attract outstanding people, and grow. In many respects, we were not traditional entrepreneurs.

We started SAI on February 3, 1969, with a couple of technical consulting contracts, one from Brookhaven National Laboratory, and the other from Los Alamos National Laboratory. I then had to make the fateful decision on whether or not to incorporate. It turns out that there are important legal protections if an organization incorporates. And after that, one thing led to another. A talented lawyer named Tom Ackerman at Gray, Cary, Ames and Frye helped me though the incorporation process. We had to figure out who would own the corporation. That was a decision I really didn't want to get into, because I didn't know anything about distributing founder stock. The only stock I'd ever owned came from some General Dynamics stock options awarded to me by Freddy de Hoffman (the founder of General Atomic and a world-renowned scientist), which became an important asset in financing the very early SAI. But I had to develop a totally new kind of stock system for this start-up enterprise. Many others who joined us knew far more about corporate stock systems than I did.

It took about $50,000 of my personal assets to start the company—a $30,000 loan to the company that was paid back to me, and a $20,000 stock investment. There were plenty of scientists and engineers available in San Diego at that time from Convair and other organizations—some from General Atomic as well—who were looking for a change. Some of those people joined us. The early SAI always paid employees a salary—which was unusual for a start-up—although mine was deferred for a year. Eventually we had cash flow problems, which is to be expected in a new company, and we needed to find additional sources of funds to maintain our operations.

Through Myron Eichen, one of San Diego's most successful entrepreneurs also with General Atomic origins, we got involved with Joe Young in the La Jolla branch of the Bank of America. Even though Joe was a great guy, he was no fool. When he lent money to the company, he wanted me to use my house as loan collateral just in case we didn't know what we were doing. And there wasn't any evidence that we did. So between the Bank of America, some cosigning on the part of the early employees who were joining us, and my own investment, we kept solvent and growing.

After a year, a surprising thing happened—we made a profit. I suspected something was the matter. We had a rather small board, and one of the board members—Harold Smith, who was and still is on the UC Berkeley faculty—said, "You know, Bob, you'd better get some help because you don't know what you're doing." All our accounting people were well trained. It's just that we couldn't believe that we had made $20,000 of profit so soon. We—being researchers—were often not exposed to profit making at our former employers.

So we brought in a highly recommended entrepreneur from the Bay Area named Art Biehl. It turned out he was not a big believer in widespread employee ownership. However, he gave us a lot of good advice. He thought like a traditional high-tech entrepreneur—he had dealt with venture capital people. He had done financing. He believed in a small number of people owning the company. He believed that people who came in after a while should get only a small piece of the company. He felt we should use venture capital financing to begin, and then take the company public. I agreed with none of this, but I listened to Art anyway because he was smart, was a real friend, and was trying hard to help us.

Art said that we should first seek a private placement to satisfy our immediate cash needs, and then do an initial public offering (IPO)—that was his recipe for success, and he'd done it successfully several times. I'm surprised the early SAI didn't go down the public track because Art was certainly exposing us to the wonders of IPOs. In addition, he made many valuable suggestions on the company's direction and specific research programs. But pushing the traditional venture approach was near the top of his list.

Something must have happened to stop me from buying into this traditional approach. I had observed that it can destroy a company, and harm all but a limited number of insiders—most often the top executives—who do very well financially. This fact usually doesn't concern most of these early employees. They may, however, feel some remorse about the fact that their original company is disappearing—being replaced by a new public company.

Joe Young was a little uneasy about us bringing in financing from another source in the early days, but Art Biehl felt strongly that we should do it, so we sold $200,000 of SAIC stock to a medical group that Davis Skaggs, a San Francisco investment banking organization, had assembled. It was one of those things you do in a start-up company. The medical group netted a 10-fold profit on their investment. I do not recommend the venture capital approach if you can avoid it because an inordinate amount of the ownership ends up with disinterested financial investors. From that point on, and with a very generous new line of credit from Joe Young and the Bank of America, we would never need to use venture capital funding again.

Clearly, SAIC's employees resonated with this unconventional, yet simple idea. In a business world where it is rare for employees—particularly employees outside of a small group of top executives and board members—to own stock in their own companies, SAIC broke the mold with an astonishing percentage of employees who owned company equity. More than 80 percent of SAIC's employees own company stock, and over 90 percent has been the historical pattern for decades.

But this figure is just the tip of the iceberg for a company that most of the time has typically flown below the radar of most business observers. By several measures, SAIC's business performance speaks for itself.

SUSTAINED BUSINESS EXPANSION AND DIVERSIFICATION

Doing business with the government is a constant challenge for contractors. The end of the Cold War altered the contracts business landscape permanently. Many defense and federal government programs were scaled back, and frequently terminated, so contractors increasingly turned to the private sector and nondefense government agencies for new income streams. SAIC met this challenge, and not only survived but thrived. As defense conversion engulfed the defense contracting community, SAIC emerged as a diversified, financially sound corporation and launched a new cycle of growth in shareholder value. Its record of rapid and consistent annual revenue growth since 1969 (See Figure 1.1) is exceptional:

- In FY1970, SAIC's first FY end, total annual revenues were $243,000.

- In FY1980, total annual revenues exceeded $150 million (90 percent CAGR, 10 years).

- In FY1990, total annual revenues exceeded $1 billion, making SAIC one of the largest employee-owned companies in the United States.

- In FY1999, total annual revenues exceeded $4.7 billion, placing SAIC on the Fortune 500 list.

- In FY2006, total annual revenues were approximately $8 billion.

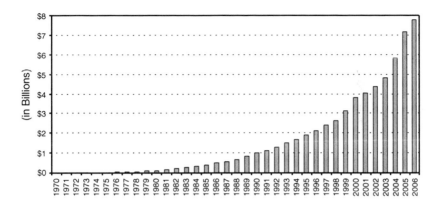

FIGURE 1.1 SAIC Revenue (1970–2006)

SAIC's FY2006 results represented the thirty-sixth year of continued revenue growth, demonstrating SAIC's position as one of the most successful employee-owned companies in the United States. Revenue and earnings grew at a compounded annual growth rate of 33 percent over this time period. SAIC grew into a Fortune 500 company within 30 years and only had three years (1998, 2001, and 2002) that resulted in single-digit annual revenue growth.

Aside from a couple of remarkable years during the dot-com boom, operating income growth was consistent with revenue growth, meaning SAIC maintained fairly consistent margins over this time period. The margins might be less than other comparable companies at any given time, since I was interested in guaranteeing future revenue growth. SAIC was in the business of selling brainpower, mostly to federal government agencies that did not generally pay high contract fees to begin with. I made a conscious decision to build SAIC around selling the expertise and smarts of our employees and not selling widgets. This meant foregoing higher profits while building significant revenue growth. Even so, SAIC never had an unprofitable year.

STEADY STOCK PRICE GROWTH— DOUBLE-DIGIT TRACK RECORD

SAIC has posted remarkable stock price growth since its founding in 1969. From the end of that first fiscal year until 2006, the company's

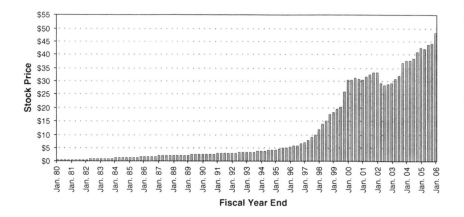

FIGURE 1.2   SAIC Stock Price: 26-Year History

stock price rose by an annualized compounded rate of 34 percent. An investment of just $100 in 1970 would be worth more than $3.5 million in 2006. And when the stock market crashed in 1987—losing 20 percent of its value—SAIC lost only 5 percent.

Consistent with its can-do, "if it doesn't exist, let's invent it" philosophy, SAIC's management team created Bull, Inc.—a wholly owned broker/dealer subsidiary, registered with the SEC and NASD, that conducted quarterly internal market trades for employees who wanted to buy or sell shares of SAIC stock. This internal market increased the liquidity of the stock while the company's steady performance kept its price moving upward in almost every quarter of the company's existence. (See Figure 1.2.)

GROWTH, MARKET LEADERSHIP, AND THE RANKINGS TO PROVE IT

While SAIC's customers and competitors in government and business closely watched SAIC's performance, this story is about a company that flew below the radar until its reputation could no longer be concealed. More than a few successful companies have copied elements of SAIC's business model. Even so, SAIC remains an enigma to many of the company's com-

petitors, and it can be very difficult to develop win strategies when competing against SAIC:

- SAIC is the largest employee-owned research and engineering firm in
  the United States, and the third largest majority employee-owned
  company in the United States, after Publix Supermarkets and Hy-Vee.
- By 1999, SAIC had joined the Fortune 500 list as number 347. Six
  years later—in 2006—SAIC reached number 285 on the Fortune
  500 list.
- *Fortune* ranked SAIC number 4 among America's most admired information technology services companies in 2006.
- *Federal Computer Week* ranked SAIC the second largest systems inte-
  grator for the federal government in 2005.

Since its founding in 1969, SAIC has had few peers in the markets serving government and private sector clients, especially compared to other privately held companies.

HERE, THERE—EVERYWHERE

My original vision of building a good place to work led to the creation of an
entrepreneurial environment that led the company to engage in numerous
remarkable business initiatives—from acquisitions to product development,
from domestic markets to global ventures. Far-ranging in their scope, some
of these business opportunities were experiments for SAIC—and some of
them succeeded beyond all reasonable expectations:

- *Defense transformation:* SAIC established a leadership role working
  closely with the Department of Defense during the Cold War, and
  then helping to transition the military and other federal agencies into
  the post-Cold War era. Today, the company develops leading-edge
  concepts, technologies, and systems to solve complex challenges facing the U.S. military and its allies in the twenty-first century, helping
  them make decisions according to new rules in a new warfare environment and transforming the way they fight.
- *Intelligence:* SAIC develops solutions to help the U.S. defense, intelligence, and homeland security communities build an integrated

intelligence picture, allowing them to become more agile and dynamic in challenging environments and produce actionable intelligence.

- *Homeland security and defense:* SAIC develops technical problem-solving approaches and provides systems integration and support services to help federal, state, local, and foreign governments and private-sector customers protect the United States and allied homelands.

- *Energy and environment:* SAIC brings science, engineering, policy, and information-management skills to some of the most difficult energy, environmental remediation, compliance, and energy infrastructure issues in the nation. Expanding beyond the early days of Superfund projects, SAIC is today a full-service environmental, health, and safety provider.

- *Logistics and product support:* SAIC provides logistics and product support to enhance the readiness and operational capability of U.S. military personnel and weapon support systems.

- *Systems engineering and integration:* SAIC provides systems engineering and integration services to help its customers design, manage, and protect complex IT networks and infrastructure.

- *Research and development:* As one of the largest science and technology contractors to the U.S. government, SAIC conducts leading-edge research and development of new technologies with applications in areas such as national security, intelligence, and life sciences.

- *Health and life sciences:* SAIC supports government and commercial customers in all phases of drug development. SAIC is the support contractor for an NCI research and development center, advances vaccine research and manufacturing, integrates disparate scientific systems, and supports regulatory affairs for drug, biological, and device products.

- *Commercial services:* SAIC helps its customers become more competitive, offering technology-driven consulting, systems integration, and outsourcing services and products in selected commercial markets, currently IT support for oil and gas exploration and production, applications and IT infrastructure management for utilities, and data life cycle management for pharmaceuticals.

Subsequent chapters explore a number of SAIC's technology and innovations—in the areas listed previously—as well as major acquisitions including Bellcore/Telcordia and Network Solutions.

A HISTORY OF INNOVATION—FOR TECHNOLOGY AND BUSINESS

SAIC's success was the result of the convergence of innovative technology and innovative business practices. When I decided to start the company, my motivation wasn't financial. I wanted to create a company that would attract talented scientists and engineers who would tackle nationally important scientific issues. And they would stay at SAIC because of the challenging problems and a work environment that encouraged creative thinking.

As this unique workplace evolved, a number of business principles and practices emerged. These principles and practices, explored in greater depth in subsequent chapters, are summarized here:

- *People first.* Over its many years, SAIC put people first—the organization was expected to serve customers, employees, and owners (who were employees), not the other way around. The basic formula worked exceedingly well: Hire very smart people, encourage their entrepreneurial spirit, let them focus on customers, and reward them for their contributions.

- *Freedom (with strings attached).* SAIC was specifically designed to be an organization where managers and employees would be free to pursue work they were passionate about—to start, operate, control, and grow their own business units under the umbrella of the parent company, and unleash their own energy and creativity. While they were encouraged to build and run their own business, employees were expected to follow company practices for bidding and contracting and adhere to the highest ethical standards in the process to protect their customers' and the company's best interests.

- *From science to solutions.* SAIC was a company founded by scientists, and it used science and engineering to provide the most effective, efficient, up-to-date, and highest quality solutions for specific client problems. The company put a premium on hiring the most talented scientists and engineers it could find, pointing them toward problems of national importance, and then getting out of the way. We believed in and valued small beginnings. As our experience showed, small things often beget large things. Although SAIC eventually performed on a wide variety of projects, science and engineering has always remained deep within the company's core.

- *Employee ownership.* If freedom of movement was the incentive that drew talented people into SAIC, then employee ownership was the glue that kept them there. SAIC built a culture firmly rooted in the simple idea that those who contribute to the company should own it, and ownership should be commensurate with a person's contribution and performance. Without employee ownership, SAIC would not exist today.

- *Participation in decision making.* At SAIC, employees were not only expected to contribute their ideas to improve the company and the services it provided, but also to make decisions that would put their ideas into action. While there was certainly a hierarchy of various managers and employees, the expectation was that decisions would be made at the lowest level possible, and problems resolved at the lowest appropriate level, thus cutting red tape and providing customers with more responsive service.

- *Organized for growth.* Bucking the traditional rigid hierarchy of its contemporaries in each of its decades of operation, SAIC created a decentralized organizational model. At SAIC, the central organization provided essential policy guidance to its various business units and exercised substantial oversight and financial control, but otherwise kept out of the way as much as possible. This approach allowed its motivated managers to build their businesses free of the kinds of administrative restraints that would have fettered their efforts in most other organizations.

- *No grand plan.* Rather than following voluminous plans that laid out company initiatives years into the future, SAIC encouraged the organization to grow organically, following the interests and instincts of its entrepreneurial program managers. While a formal planning process was eventually put into place to ensure the most efficient use of company resources, flexibility and initiative were always considered more important than slavish adherence to "the plan."

- *Everyone a salesperson.* From its earliest days, SAIC's leadership put a premium on hiring scientists and engineers who didn't just do the work, but who also were responsible for selling the work. By enlisting the people who did the work in the selling process, SAIC kept close tabs on emerging customer needs, developed particularly close relationships with customers, and minimized the overhead expense that would have been required to hire and fund a large separate selling organization. Everyone in the company was expected to keep his or her eyes open for new work, and was rewarded for successes.

- *Extensive feedback and lessons learned.* SAIC put a formal "lessons learned" process into place to gather together feedback from employees who were directly involved in new initiatives or particularly complex programs, bringing insights to light and recording them for others to learn from. A variety of different meetings—the most important known as Management Council that occurred during the company's quarterly Meetings Week—created even more opportunities for obtaining feedback and learning lessons. These learning-based processes became essential features of SAIC's proposal review strategies as well.

- *Experiment constantly.* One of the hallmarks of SAIC has been the willingness of its leaders to constantly experiment with new business entities, corporate structures, and staff. To encourage experiments, managers at all levels of the company were annually given control over pockets of money (called "guidelines") that they could use to invest in growing their own organization. The extraordinary degree to which discretionary money and decision making were delegated to managers at the division level—the lowest level of the company—and all levels in between that level and the CEO, is unprecedented in the defense industry and rare for *any* business.

- *Expect reasonable profit, but with stock price growth.* While projects, divisions, and groups had to be profitable, the plan for profitability (as measured by margin percentage) at SAIC was generally lower than at most other companies of its kind. The company's values and financial model placed much greater emphasis on steady growth, customer satisfaction, and advancing the nation's interests rather than on squeezing its clients for every last dime.

- *Governance—sustainability or transition?* Numerous laws and regulations—recent and not so recent—are making corporate governance more time consuming than ever, while increasing the costs of doing business and hamstringing the ability of organizations to act quickly to seize opportunities as they may arise. SAIC's board of directors has long faced the challenge of positioning the company for the future while maintaining the values that made SAIC great—all while keeping up to date on the latest regulatory issues. SAIC's board was an important asset—useful not only in an advisory role, but as a key instrument of growth. To these ends, members were recruited who could help the company achieve both its short- and long-term goals.

In the chapters that follow, we consider how each of these principles and practices led to SAIC's extraordinary success, and how the lessons that we learned over the years can help you create your own business success stories if you are so inclined. Finally, in Chapter 14, I take a look at the future of employee ownership, American business competitiveness, science and technology, and SAIC. As you will see, there is much to be hopeful about, and much work to be done.

2

The Culture: People First

SAIC places a very high value on staff productivity. We have endeavored to maintain a reasonable cost structure and to make the best people available to the customer. Also, SAIC's organizational structure plays a key role in productivity by minimizing layers of management and decision making in order to focus on responding to its customers.

—from *Principles and Practices of SAIC*

Over the years, many people have asked me what the "secret sauce" was that turned a small science and engineering firm called SAIC into the remarkable, diversified business success that it is today. If you could boil down the SAIC sauce to its essentials, what ingredients would remain?

While some say it's the company's entrepreneurial culture, and others say it's employee ownership, I personally believe that the secret sauce behind SAIC's success is the *people*—the employees. It is creating an environment that allows individuals to make a difference and be recognized for it.

THE MEANING OF PEOPLE FIRST

Early on, my philosophy was to hire excellent and motivated employees, give them freedom to build the business around their interests, and reward them in keeping with their contribution to the overall success of the company. I wanted "triple threat" people—that is, women and men who (1) could market and sell the work, (2) who were leading technical experts in their fields and could do the work, and (3) could help manage the work and the people who performed it.

To me, putting people first did not mean doling out high, uncompetitive salaries and benefits, extravagant perks and office arrangements, or total independence from oversight and management direction. One fundamental tension posed within a start-up, people-centric business is how to provide financial and psychic rewards that keep employees motivated and glued into the company while remaining within generally constrained resources. Furthermore, as we grew in size, not everyone could be a triple threat employee, nor could we rely totally on every employee to always be responsible or share our values. But we still needed motivated employees in every corner of the company, and we needed proper, legal, and ethical behavior and ways to monitor their performance.

These objectives often imposed conflicting requirements. Freedom does not always bring with it responsible, ethical behavior or a positive bottom line. Bureaucratic oversight does not sit well with impatient entrepreneurs who want something done right *now*. Reasonable pay and benefits do not always satisfy high-performing, hard-charging people. Psychic rewards are highly variable in the eye of the beholder. Our approaches took many forms and evolved over time.

First, we needed to allow our managers the freedom of action to run their businesses; that is, hire and fire, market their people and services, reward employees, and invest in their marketing and technology bases. Over time, we developed relatively simple accounting and reporting metrics and methods, and we granted to the division manager (the lowest level where profits and losses were recorded for the company) the ability to trade bottom-line profit margin for investment, as long as he or she met our modest profit margin goals. There is more about our specific financial approaches later in this book.

Second, the development of an incentive and stock ownership system (with all the bells and whistles that evolved as we became more sophisticated) was another critical element. It eventually evolved into a system that dealt not only with the superstars but also with the employees whose performance was not as stellar, but good nonetheless. This system included stock awards, cash awards, stock options, and direct purchase of company stock, a system to distribute the rewards in an equitable way, and a means to provide liquidity to those who needed it. All of this had to be carried out in compliance with the regulations of almost every state, the U.S. Securities and Exchange Commission (SEC), and the National Association of Securities Dealers (NASD). In order for these incentives to be meaningful and motivate the desired behavior, long-term increases in the stock price were required. This was particularly true for stock options, which for most of our history were not a charge to our bottom line under the accounting rules. Further, over time, employees were able to accumulate sufficient wealth through prior stock purchases and awards to use appreciated stock to help pay for later stock option exercises. The creation and the orchestration of all these moving parts took a good deal of time and thought. But it is the structure on which the company was built. There is more on the stock ownership system in Chapter 5.

Recognition of outstanding performance was also essential. For example, we extensively used titles, face time with upper managers and board members, participation in company policy development, committee work, participation in outside professional organizations, awards for technical and administrative excellence, and more to address the softer side of putting people first. In this context, I felt obliged to keep in touch with as many people in the organization as made sense and where it helped me do my job. Chain of command was not important to me in the context of putting people first, and this no doubt rubbed some managers the wrong way. But speaking with employees at all levels of the organization gave me an unfiltered perspective on the pulse of the company and access to the employees most knowledgeable about particular issues. I have found that many of our best people were less motivated by money than with doing something of lasting value, and recognition is an essential element of this ethos.

And, finally, as an integral part of providing psychic rewards, I felt it was my job to set high standards and serious, worthwhile objectives for the overall company. We really wanted to make a difference to the nation as a company and as individuals. The best way we could do that was by solving challenging technical problems that others might not or could not tackle. This was not rhetoric, and this strong desire helped us get some excellent people into the company who would make a difference.

A HIERARCHY OF IDEAS

There can be no doubt that SAIC's science-focused, entrepreneurial culture attracted a unique individual—talented, motivated, smart, and energetic self-starters who thrived on the freedom they found in this company. In a business world where "no" (and its related variants) is the most common response to those who want to push an organization's limits or embark on initiatives that are even slightly outside the box, SAIC was a place where employees knew that as long as what they wanted to do wasn't illegal or unethical—and as long as the work was important and there was a possibility of making some money or covering an employee's labor cost—then it was much more likely they would hear the words "why not?"

SAIC was first and foremost a science and technology company. This organizational fact of life helped to spawn a culture where important decisions were made less on the basis of emotion and gut feeling and more on the basis of analysis and scientific deliberation. Says Clint Kelly (who I hired in 1988 to run the corporate-level independent research and development program for SAIC):

> An important characteristic that really set SAIC apart from other companies was that we were run by technical people—not just by business development people, MBAs, lawyers, and financial people. That is rather remarkable, and it was instrumental in the development of the company's technical culture. There are, of course, many companies that are headed by a person with a technical background, but I'll bet very few exist where technical people at every level actually run the company—that is, make the decisions that count, and where those decisions are based on the kind of analytical reasoning employed by scientists and engineers.

In many ways, SAIC in its early days was like the government laboratories from which many of its scientist-employees were drawn—except that the company was definitely in business to make a profit. There was a formal hierarchy—CEO, vice presidents, managers, and all the rest—based on titles and positions in the organization, but *what* you knew was far more important than your title. SAIC's real hierarchy was predominantly one of ideas and knowledge, and managing and growing the company was primarily the province of its scientists and technologists—a task for which they were uniquely suited in this company dedicated to taking science to solutions.

In essence, SAIC was a meritocracy—a place that rewarded and advanced employees up the ladder of success based on their performance. That was important to me. If you won the work, you owned it and were responsible for delivering and growing the business. To further emphasize the company's culture of entrepreneurial leadership, organizational units were often referred to by the last name of the leader. This was our way at the beginning, and it remained so as the company grew into a multimillion-dollar organization. So the successes and failures were directly attributed to a specific person, not a faceless organizational unit.

SAIC placed a premium on ideas—this was one of the things that made us different and helped us stand out from the competition. Highly motivated people prefer to work with other highly motivated people and at companies that recognize their talents, allow these talents to be applied liberally, and then reward them when they succeed. They also prefer to work for companies that have a low tolerance for people who are not motivated to achieve, and that act quickly to weed these people out of the organization when there is no fit. There's nothing worse to a high-achiever than a manager who tolerates low-achievers—and they usually aren't afraid to seek out organizations that set the bar high.

Because we believed in the ability of individuals to make a difference, when we recruited new employees to join our team, we put that quality—the drive to take initiative and to make a difference for customers and for the company— above many others. We assumed that if you hired the right people and gave them the authority they needed to do their jobs well, then they would do the right things. If we were wrong in our estimation of someone's inner drive or ability, then it usually didn't take long for them to realize that SAIC wasn't the best place for them and leave. If they didn't come to this realization for themselves and take action to exit the company, then we helped them on their way.

It was hard to hide manager nonperformance at SAIC. Managers were expected to contribute value—primarily by bringing new business into the company—and to exhibit common sense in meeting their financial goals. And we kept a close eye on the managers to ensure that this expectation was met. Not only that, but it became a responsibility of all employees to be alert for coworkers who were not contributing, and to either help them remedy this situation or ensure that management was informed so that action could be taken. Our most effective (and most highly regarded and rewarded) managers worked well with customers to build the business, rolled-up their sleeves to fix problems, and knew their business in great enough detail to be able to anticipate technical as well as business issues. There was an informal saying at SAIC that the company was one of the few places where you could fire your boss in the case of his or her misconduct or poor performance. This was not true in a literal sense— lower-level employees could not terminate higher-level employees—but we listened to our employees and took action when necessary.

ATTRACTING TALENTED HIGH ACHIEVERS (AND KEEPING THEM)

If there's one thing that has become apparent to most managers over the past decade, it's that the most important resource they have at their command is their *human* capital. I knew that SAIC would survive and thrive only if we were able to attract the most talented people, and then keep them happy once they signed on with the company. Frankly, an average worker might not thrive as an SAIC employee. We demanded a lot from our employees, and we specifically sought out the men and women who we thought could provide the mix of skills and experience that we needed to grow the company. The company's hiring strategy was an effective one: recruit men and women who were veterans in their fields, as well as the most promising new college graduates and trainees. Our culture was tolerant of iconoclasts and employees who didn't strictly conform. We felt that employees could and should have fun and not take themselves too seriously.

SAIC employees felt appreciated because they knew that if they did their jobs (and did them well), they would be noticed and taken care of by the company—professionally in terms of challenging career assignments, and financially through compensation and stock ownership appreciation. As a result, the company's unique culture—and its emphasis on employee ownership, freedom, and entrepreneurship—exerted a powerful gravitational pull, drawing the most talented people to the company.

Employee ownership provided a magnet for a certain class of individuals—very technically competent men and women who wanted a good place to work. These people represented a particular type of entrepreneur—not quite as entrepreneurial as those who would go out on their own and start up companies out of nothing (although some did), but considerably more entrepreneurial than many who were working in aerospace or large defense companies at that time. We were able to attract and provide an environment for employees who could then work on the company's interests as well as their own, but in a secure environment that offered professional and financial growth. With corporate, group, business unit, and operation administration taking the burden of running most administrative functions off of their shoulders, many of them thought they had found a very special place to work.

Making this culture work required finding the right kind of people, and then making sure they were in the right positions within the company. If they weren't, then I had no qualms moving them around until they were in a place that was the best match for their skills and talents. Says Sydell Gold (who joined SAIC in 1992, worked with Steve Rockwood as a deputy sector manager for research and development, and led account management for the Defense Threat Reduction Agency):

> People were so important to Bob. He took an interest in all kinds of individuals and he let them find the job that they were best suited for and that they wanted to do. It wasn't as if the organization had a bunch of slots that needed to be filled, and then you tried to force people into them. He had a wide range of connections throughout industry and the government, and when he saw somebody that he thought would be useful and intelligent, or would bring some dimension that SAIC didn't have or needed, he took a personal interest in hiring them.

It was one thing to get recruits to join the company, and it was another thing altogether to get them to stay for a long period of time. But, according to Gene Ray, who joined SAIC in July 1970, and ultimately went on to found his own successful venture, the Titan Corporation, SAIC had figured out how to keep these very talented employees happy—and loyal. Says Ray, who stayed with the company for 11 years:

> I think there were two things that kept people there. One was an incentive package that rewarded employees who performed—it was rewards based on performance, and that was mainly in equity in the company. SAIC never overpaid in salary, and by far the most underpaid person in the company the whole time I was there was Bob Beyster. He shared ownership of the company very widely, and that was used to help recruit, and then encourage them to stay. The second thing was the decentralized way the company was run, but with tight financial controls. Bob always knew exactly what was going on within the company, but he also delegated responsibility for running the business to the people who worked for him.

Much to my consternation, it didn't take long for SAIC's talented employees to become very popular recruiting targets for much of the company's competition and by those companies that were on the lookout for individuals who would become immediate assets. Almost every senior manager received offers to jump ship during their SAIC careers, and retaining them became a pivotal part of my role in much the same way that I had been instrumental in their recruitment.

Whenever a key person at SAIC decided to leave, he or she could be certain that SAIC would mount a spirited counteroffer campaign. Instead of telling them that they were making a good decision for themselves and wishing them well in their new career path, I and other SAIC managers let them know that the job they were about to leave was a better one. In some cases, a new job situation at SAIC was developed to accommodate the employee's goals. In some cases, good employees were convinced to stay—continuing their contributions to the company. In other cases, they left anyway. But, whatever the outcome, in more than a few cases, our efforts paid off for both of us when key talent stayed with us and went on to make even greater contributions to the company and more rewards for themselves.

Steve Rizzi (who joined SAIC in 1984 and runs a 250-person information technology laboratory providing solutions to federal intelligence and life sciences agencies) explained how going the extra mile in saving an employee who was about to leave had a long-term impact on the company. Says Rizzi:

> I remember when one of my key managers told me that he was leaving. I called San Diego and Bob met with him a couple of days later, after I flew my guy out there from DC. The magic worked—my guy stayed, and he's still with the company today. This sort of thinking also rubbed off on those of us who paid attention to Bob's technique. I remember wanting one guy so badly that I went over to his house on the weekend and helped him watch his three young kids—all under five years old—because it was the only time we could meet to discuss our job offer. That guy is still here, too. That sort of caring and personal attention is what breeds loyalty.

THE BEYSTER BOOK

I learned many useful things when working at General Atomic, which had a positive impact on my management skills at SAIC. I kept massive notes on ideas from meetings I attended and on conversations I had during my daily lunchtime run with friends and associates. We were prone to have good business ideas during these occasions and I wrote them in my "Beyster Book" immediately, lest they be lost. This pocket notebook saved my neck for at least 40 years. Each notebook lasted for one month or so because I would embellish ideas while I waited for appointments. Recruiting of staff, bonus reminders, phone calls to make, and more went into the Beyster Book. All of these actions are probably doable now on your cell phone. My philosophy on this matter is that some information is so valuable that it is important not to take a chance on your memory. This way of keeping track of ideas, information, and things to do lasted until the day I left SAIC. And to some extent it still does.

RECRUITING: THE PERSONAL TOUCH

In the early days of the company, it was a challenge to recruit individuals to join such a speculative, new enterprise. It was a small business then, with all the risks associated with start-ups. Although SAIC was growing, there was no telling if growth would slow down or even stop in any given year, or the next, or whether the company's new recruits would have jobs in six months. We had no track record. How could we convince them to leave their current comfortable jobs to become entrepreneurs and part of a company that they owned and where they would be listened to?

I often pushed the balance in SAIC's favor by becoming personally involved in recruiting talented employees, getting on the phone with candidates or inviting them in for personal interviews or to make an offer of employment. More than a few candidates were surprised when I joined in the interview process for key technical hires at the individual contributor level. This was an uncommon practice for other companies the size of SAIC, and it made a lasting impression on recruits and employees. This direct and personal touch brought us many talented employees, a significant number of whom built successful careers with the company.

Key prospects had to run the gauntlet of five or more interviewers. This screening process ensured that SAIC hired the best in class, because only the most talented and motivated to work for the company survived the process.

For those survivors, the rewards could arrive quickly. Sometimes I was so convinced that a certain person should join the company that I was willing to back up my belief by offering a piece of my own financial stake in the company to enhance the incentive offer. In the early days of the company, I optioned some of my own stock to recruits, essentially betting on their ability to bring in enough business to give me and SAIC a satisfactory return on our investment. Sometimes they did—and sometimes they didn't. But either way, I would do everything in my power to land a key employee when his or her experience and future promise justified it, and other managers picked up on this behavior, becoming personally involved in the hiring process themselves.

We also took time to analyze our new hires to try to understand exactly what drove them personally. We became proficient at detecting the core motivators for these high-achieving self-starters. For example, some people wanted to do technical work or policy analysis, and they weren't interested in becoming managers. Others wanted to get into marketing and grow the company, while others wanted to manage projects. I then attempted whenever possible to put employees in positions that matched their motivations, even reorganizing the company to fill positions that would fully engage them.

What these employees also recognized was that I accommodated those whose motivations changed as their careers progressed. Former managers became principal investigators; principal investigators became committee chairs and worked on special corporate needs. As the company grew, the opportunities to explore new assignments also grew. I not only allowed this to happen but also actively encouraged it.

TURNING POINT: SPACE AND WEATHER PROGRAMS (NASA/NOAA)

SAIC had a unique philosophy when it came to contracts—almost any size contract was acceptable, so long as it could help provide coverage for someone's salary while making a profit, however modest. While competitors might turn their noses up at relatively small-dollar contracts, this was rarely a problem for us. Why? Partly because such contracts not only provided coverage and profit, but also because we realized that small programs were often technical stepping-stones to much larger programs, we proved ourselves to our customers and became increasingly important to their success. As our expansion into space programs showed, this philosophy sometimes led to significant opportunities for the company.

When Neil Hutchinson joined SAIC in 1989 as a corporate vice president, after 25 years at the National Aeronautics and Space Administration (NASA) and a short stint at Rockwell International, the company had only a few contracts with the national space agency. Before joining SAIC, Neil worked as a flight controller during the Apollo missions, eventually becoming a flight director and running Mission Control at the Johnson Space Center in Houston, Texas. There he helped bring the last astronauts back from the moon safely, ran all three Skylab flights and Apollo-Soyuz, and helped get the space station program up and running.

We had tried for years to build a major program area within NASA, but our success was limited. Ed Straker's environment and energy management sector (at the time, a sector was the highest-level organizational unit within SAIC, being comprised of a number of groups—which were themselves comprised of divisions) had a modest contract with NASA headquarters, and a handful of smaller contracts with some of NASA's field centers. At the same time, sector manager Bruce Gordon was pulling out the stops to enter the human spaceflight business. Breaking into the insular human spaceflight business would, however, require hiring the right person—someone who could make something big out of SAIC's scattered NASA efforts.

Bruce Gordon was certain he had found the right person when he hired Neil Hutchinson away from Rockwell International, where Hutchinson had gone after leaving NASA. Says Hutchinson, "This was in the late 1980s, early 1990s. I started at SAIC with a group of 75 people and a $9 million contract at NASA headquarters."

Soon after Hutchinson arrived, however, Bruce Gordon retired, SAIC lost its human spaceflight training bid, and the Gordon Sector—Hutchinson's home base—began to splinter. Neil was assigned to work directly for me, where he was given the task of figuring out how to build a significant, long-term NASA business. Hutchinson decided to target NASA's Mission to Planet Earth program—a collection of unmanned satellites that would gather data and information about the Earth's systems over a long period of time—and kicked off a series of internal SAIC meetings to develop ways we could help NASA succeed in its mission.

Success came soon. Says Neil, "One thing led to another, and we found an atmospheric sciences support contract at NASA Langley that was coming up to bid. We immersed ourselves in the competition—really poured our hearts into it—and won the contract in 1991. It was the largest NASA win in SAIC's history up to that time—$150 million total, 10 years at $15 million a year. It instantly tripled the size of the company's assistance to NASA and it became the foundation that got the Group started."

One key to winning this work away from the incumbent contractors was giving Hutchinson and his team the authority to do things differently than they had been done before, and the autonomy to act quickly—surprising the well-entrenched incumbents. Hutchinson and his team decided the key to winning the NASA bid would have to also be financial—SAIC had to deliver a top-notch technical team, but at a lower price than the competition. Hutchinson says, "We got together with the financial guys and figured out a way to bid superior technical support at a lower overhead structure. I got a lot of help from a lot of people and, as a result, we won in 1991. The work we did with these rate structures was a forerunner of the financial structure that we used over and over again to build the business. We became extremely competitive with the other companies that were operating in the market space."

But Hutchinson didn't stop there—he continued to press his advantage, leveraging his original set of small contracts into a very large business area. To keep on top of the fast-moving market, Hutchinson ran a set of internal meetings on the topic of NASA's broader goals. These meetings helped further develop the company's NASA business, as well as work with a number of other federal government agencies—including a 10-year, $500 million National Oceanic and Atmospheric Administration (NOAA) contract for the National Data Buoy Center in Mississippi. SAIC builds the buoys, maintains them, retrieves and validates the data from them, and then feeds that data into the supercomputer models used for developing weather predictions around the world. This network of buoys is also part of a tsunami early warning system.

The science developed under these contracts led to important solutions—the development of large, complex models of oceans and the atmosphere that became integral to weather forecasting and global change research in the 1990s—as well as additional, high-dollar contracts. These complex models require massive computing power, and SAIC has run two of the largest supercomputer systems in the world since the early 1990s—one at NOAA and one at NASA. By hiring the right person, we were able to turn a small business area into a very large one. Neil Hutchinson became a group manager, running his operation for more than 12 years until he stepped down in 2004.

3

The Vision:
Freedom (with
Strings Attached)

SAIC has always provided its employees with more freedom to pursue their interests and professional careers than do most other companies. All parts of SAIC (even the more tightly managed entities) are far from the lockstep organizations with which we often find ourselves competing. Responsible individuals in the company use this freedom to conduct their business with a straightforward, generally decentralized approach to matters. Avoidance of strict conformity within SAIC has fostered the growth of one of the strongest professional staffs ever assembled in the United States.

—from *Principles and Practices of SAIC*

Freedom is the catalyst that allows creativity and innovation to flourish, and it creates bonds within an organization that are strong and long lasting. The counterpoint is controlling risk and achieving financial accountability within such a freedom-oriented culture, while assuring that all employees operate legally and ethically—all within a diverse, spread-out organization that posed constant span-of-control challenges.

SAIC'S CULTURE OF FREEDOM

Absolutely central to SAIC's culture of freedom was my belief that if people are doing important work—both to them, and to the organization—and so long as they can avoid harming anyone else (while staying within budget and complying with legal requirements), then they should be free to pursue their work as they wish. This culture of freedom was the license that entrepreneurs have used to operate at SAIC for more than three decades, and it unleashed a flood of ideas from employees at all levels throughout the entire organization. According to Steve Rockwood (who left an executive position at the Los Alamos National Laboratory to join SAIC and became a strong leader in the company as an SAIC research and development sector manager and was an active and supportive member of the board of directors) the company's unique culture made it a very special place to work. Says Rockwood:

> There was a sense of a company where the values were focused on solving important problems for the nation, and the freedom to make some decisions about what was important and how you would do it. You had some control in your life. If you are going to have a lot of freedom and autonomy within your operations, you need people who are competent and able to handle that degree of responsibility. I think being a technical company helped in the sense that we attracted people who were, by training, able to handle some autonomy. Plus, working for the government was important because it protected us with its own bureaucracy. The government has all sorts of procurement laws and rules—it's very structured—so an ethical employee in a remote location of the company couldn't create a deal so horrible that it would from a pure business perspective kill the company outright. There were lots of natural checks in the system.

The freedom that managers enjoyed in the organization was expressed in many different ways. For example, division managers were allowed to decide whether to invest excess funds to cover their overhead and bid and proposal needs, or to recognize the funds as bottom-line division profit. They were also given wide-ranging autonomy to use bonuses and stock options as effective tools to motivate their employees.

As long as SAIC's line managers operated within broadly defined business criteria—ethics, contract compliance, sales, profitability, and so forth—they had the freedom to tailor their business operations in whatever way they saw fit to best satisfy their customers' needs. For example, when the U.S. Air Force identified an urgent requirement to enhance the training of B-1B bomber aircrews, SAIC's Aeronautical Systems Operation (ASO) was able to respond quickly, promptly hiring the talent and configuring the necessary resources for this $20 million project. ASO's authority to act decisively and responsibly was key not only to the ultimate success of this project, but it also led to the expansion and spin-off of related technology and products, the creation of new markets and customers, and the recruitment of very talented employees.

FREEDOM OF THOUGHT, BUT WITH STRINGS ATTACHED

The culture of freedom was buried deep within SAIC's corporate DNA, but with freedom came responsibility. On the flip side of freedom were very tight fiscal controls, which served to direct where people spent their time while limiting the company's exposure to financial risk if one or more projects got into trouble.

Intellectual freedom was valued, but not at any cost. Employees were expected to weigh financial, customer, organizational, and other implications of their decisions. According to SAIC's Peter Stocks, who joined SAIC in the late 1990s to run the U.K. operations, the flip side of the wide-ranging freedom allowed at SAIC was an intense, almost scientific scrutiny of ideas to see if they had merit in order to decide whether they should be implemented. Says Stocks:

> There was a notion that everybody had the right to have a smart idea but, equally, the company should rigorously test every idea. This unusual approach is seldom present in companies. It's a real encouragement for everybody to innovate, and a real encouragement for employees at all levels to bounce ideas off one another. Everyone knew that the scrutiny would be very rigorous and scientific, so those proposing ideas would do their homework before they brought them forward. It was really in many ways a scientist's view of the world of business.

This thought is echoed by Steve Rockwood, who has worked with hundreds of SAIC employees over the years. According to Rockwood, the system worked. You hired talented people who would (hopefully) exercise good judgment. When they occasionally veered outside the boundaries of sound financial practice, then SAIC's leaders knew that the solution was to focus on the problem *individual,* not to construct new rules or processes that would slow everyone else down by taking away *their* freedom to act. Says Rockwood:

> You don't want anarchy, so there's got to be a balance between absolute freedom and the responsibility to be a corporate citizen. That's a tough balancing act. It comes down to the people you bring in and the extent to which they exercise mature judgment and in some way understand the corporate objectives well enough to know when they've gone out of bounds. Occasionally we would have problems with people going off and doing crazy things. I think the trick is to know that generally, when that happens, you replace the person instead of adding excessive controls and management infrastructure that reduces everyone's freedom to think and to act. When you react by adding controls then, ultimately, you end up with such a rigid and stagnant system that nothing happens.

The trick then is to find the right kind of people for your business—men and women who thrive in an environment where they are expected to define their own roles rather than have them defined for them. We had to recruit people who had the confidence to think for themselves. People who needed to be told what to do in all situations did not last long. Not everyone fits in an organization like this, but when you do find the right kind of people, the organization that results can be extremely effective.

TECHNOLOGY SPOTLIGHT: NUCLEAR WEAPONS EFFECTS

One of SAIC's very first contracts—in the amount of $70,000—was with an obscure Department of Defense agency with the intriguing name of the Defense Atomic Support Agency (DASA). This agency—later renamed the Defense Nuclear Agency (DNA) and, today, the Defense Threat Reduction Agency (DTRA)—was directly descended from World War II's Manhattan Project, which designed, tested, and successfully detonated the world's first atomic bomb. The contract reflected both my interests and expertise and those of SAIC's initial group of physicist-employees.

The project itself involved calculating the spectrum of gamma rays, neutrons, and X-rays released by an exploding nuclear weapon. Our job was to straighten out the differences between the actual measurement and theory for nuclear radiation yields. When a nuclear blast occurs, blast and thermal energy is released, along with gamma rays, neutrons, and X-rays. It's a very tricky computer science job to understand the complex physics involved. The Department of Energy labs perform this function, although they didn't find it to be particularly exciting. I thought it was important, however—and DASA did, too—so they funded contracts that Bill Scott, Don Huffman, Howard Wilson, Bud Piott, Dave Hall, Jerry Pomraning, and others worked on. There weren't many measurements of the quantities involved available to us. We mainly used one-dimensional codes to first predict the neutron, gamma ray, and X-ray spectra. For the more difficult geometries, we then used two-dimensional codes for enhanced predictions. We picked weapons that were important to the underground nuclear test program and tried where possible to compare them against previous results. For weapons of interest, we compiled our results with results from Los Alamos and Lawrence Livermore Labs. We then also calculated the gamma ray and neutron spectra for several specialized weapons, which were of interest in predicting electromagnetic pulse effects. It was extremely important to get these results right. As it turns out, this subject is of recurring interest for electromagnetic pulse (EMP) prediction even today. As we added people, this capability grew and broadened.

RECRUITING AND RETAINING THE RIGHT PEOPLE FOR A CULTURE OF FREEDOM

My management team and I realized that if we hired the right people to begin with, the problems with having a culture of freedom would be minimized. There would always be a few bad apples who would try to game or take advantage of the system, but these would be the exception rather than the rule. They could be quickly identified and dealt with. The employee handbook, *Principles and Practices of SAIC,* described the company's expectations for its employees:

Most organizations have solved the problem of risk from individuals by severely curtailing freedoms. That is not SAIC's intention. Rather, we will continue to strive for a free and open company environment for the majority of our employees by limiting freedom of decision for those with poor judgment and by removing incurable cases. Moreover, because we are committed to minimizing administrative or technical bureaucracy, no one should be considered free from constructive criticism and the search for better ways to run our business.

I was usually able to find people who wanted to work in an environment that put such a high premium on freedom. Jim Russell—who started at SAIC in 1972 as its original information technology expert, quickly became one of the company's executives, and led many significant initiatives for the company including a key role on Composite Health Care System (CHCS; our first billion-dollar contract award)—states that the main reason he wanted to work for SAIC was because of its unique culture—a key part of which was freedom. The promise of employee ownership didn't hurt though. Says Russell:

> That's what I was after—freedom to do the work and build the work I wanted to do, in a setting that was attractive, and working with other people who were smart and motivated as entrepreneurs. And also to be able to get some financial gain commensurate with the hard work I would invest in the company. These principles have pretty well proved out over time. Now, it wasn't that there weren't some tough times—there were—and frustrations just like any other place. But what really counted was being appreciated and the camaraderie of working with a group of highly motivated, like-minded people.

ETHICS: DOING THINGS RIGHT

As we have seen, SAIC's culture was a very strong draw for talented, high-achieving people. However, this was not just because they would be able to work with similarly talented people, although this reason was particularly strong. Another key reason was because they would be able to work for an organization that put ethical behavior at the top of its list. Talented and motivated people were attracted to us because we were trying to do things right.

Doing things right was the consistent message from the very top of the organization. I always felt strongly that it was SAIC's duty to provide its customers with the very best and highest-quality services—at a fair price and a reasonable profit. Providing customers with half-baked solutions was simply not acceptable to me, nor was gouging a customer or taking advantage of them in any way. Ethical breaches resulted in severe penalties, and were often grounds for termination.

Ethical problems and issues were addressed in a variety of ways in hopes of encouraging full employee disclosure and transparency. We always encouraged employees to report and resolve ethics problems with their immediate supervisors or a local human resources manager. But we also knew that because employees might be reticent to speak to their supervisor about a problem, we opened up other avenues for reporting and resolving ethics problems, including an ethics hotline and the Employee Ethics Committee. If none of these avenues worked for an employee, then I encouraged them to contact me directly.

The Employee Ethics Committee—which comprised 25 employees from many different company locations—played a major role in the development of guidelines for ethical employee behavior. For example, when it was discovered in the 1980s that a small group of employees was not charging time in strict accordance with the rules (government contracts require precise time charging so that federally appropriated dollars are spent in the ways for which they were intended), the situation was identified and the charges were corrected. However, SAIC's Employee Ethics Committee decided that the company should go a step further, by clearly spelling out for employees the behavior expected of them. I agreed with this assessment. This led to the development of the SAIC credo, which formalized our high ethical expectations for employees.

SAIC CREDO

We, as Science Applications International Corporation employees, are dedicated to the delivery of quality scientific and technical products and services contributing to the security and well-being of our nation and the free world. We believe high ethical standards are essential to achievement of our individual corporate goals. As such, we fully subscribe to the following commitments:

TO OUR CUSTOMERS

We shall place the highest priority on the quality, timeliness, and competitiveness of our products and services.

We shall pursue our objectives with a commitment to personal integrity and high professional standards.

TO OUR FELLOW EMPLOYEES, PRESENT, AND PROSPECTIVE

We shall promote an environment that encourages new ideas, high-quality work, and professional achievement.

We shall treat our fellow employees honestly and fairly; and we shall ensure equal opportunity for employment and advancement.

We shall share the rewards of success with those whose honest efforts contribute to that success.

TO OUR NEIGHBORS

We shall be responsible citizens, respecting the laws and customs of each community in which we live or conduct our business.

TO OUR SHAREHOLDERS

We shall conduct ourselves so as to enhance and preserve the reputation of the company.

Consistent with the commitments expressed above, we shall strive to provide our shareholders a fair return on investment.

TURNING POINT: COMPANYWIDE INITIATIVES

In many ways, SAIC was a loose federation of businesses held together by tight corporate financial controls. While these tight financial controls exerted a lot of power over our many divisions, we realized that this would not be enough to have the desired effect. As we grew, we needed new companywide initiatives to bring this loose organization together. The reasons for this were many, including opening up channels of communication, encouraging teaming on contract bids, promoting our policies and practices, investing to establish technology leadership, keeping up with new client initiatives and news, leveraging the corporate functions, and simply just providing our employees with the sense that they were a part of a larger company. We accomplished this by instituting a variety of companywide initiatives, for example: Meetings Week, the Proposal Center, the Technical Environment Committee, SAIC University, Division Manager's Forum, and SAIC's intranet—Information Source for Science Applications International Corporation (ISSAIC).

The original name of SAIC's Meetings Week was "Hell Week"—I presume based on the duration and intensity of the business meetings that occurred.

Meetings Week was unique to SAIC, and it had a huge impact on the company's long-term success. Meetings Week was an event—scheduled four times a year—set aside specifically for conducting formal and informal meetings that would further communication and the development of the company. This forum provided us with a way to get the geographically dispersed parts of the company together to discuss marketing, technical capabilities, teaming, recruiting, incentives, policy and procedures, and other topics; and the candor and breadth of the discussion helped define SAIC's personality.

Meetings Weeks were held in different locations around the country where SAIC had a major presence—most often in San Diego or McLean, Virginia but sometimes in other locations, including Norfolk (AMSEC), New Jersey (Telcordia), Annapolis, and others.

A typical agenda would be jammed with nonstop meetings of a number of SAIC committees and groups—including the Incentives Committee, Management Council, Risk Committee, Group Marketing Coordinators, Technical Environment Committee, Employee Ethics Committee, Software Working Group, and more—as well as meetings on technical and other areas of company interest, such as corporate telecommunications, directed energy weapons, NASA's Mission to Planet Earth program, and supercomputers. In later years, there was a large employee-training component. Once a year there was a company-wide awards ceremony to recognize outstanding employee performance.

Management Council usually met on Thursday morning of Meetings Week. This meeting included formal presentations about the company's financial health, marketing performance and plans, lessons learned, and policy issues. In essence, it was a quarterly assessment of *everything* about SAIC—good and bad—and it was shared with everyone, including employees, customers, and even competitors. It was here that I assessed our recent and ongoing successes and challenges, provided my views on what things I felt were most important for the company's future, and suggestions for where we should focus our attention.

At Management Councils during the 1990s, it was not uncommon for as many as 1,500 people to attend. On Thursday evenings, there was a pre-board dinner held for board members, guests, and invited employees of the company, for which we generally had an outside speaker who was often a prominent government official. Board committees such as the Audit Committee and Ethics and Audit Committee met on Thursdays, and the full board met on Friday mornings and went through its quarterly business meetings, a key component of which was the setting of SAIC's stock price for the coming quarter.

In the early days of the company, there were no videoconferencing capabilities or even large-scale conference calls, so this week of meetings served to open channels of communication and to develop rapport between groups and individuals that needed to work together. This was the time when deals were cut between internal organizations regarding future business development and when the multiple committees in the company got together to formulate and brief their results to interested managers. It was also a time when I made decisions about the allocation of discretionary resources to managers who needed them—my famous "guidelines." It was also a time when customers and potential new employees and teammates were invited to participate and get to know us better, where vendors had a chance to demonstrate their wares, and where SAIC divisions could showcase their technical capabilities.

Of necessity, the form of Meetings Week changed over the years as we grew—more structure, more process, more formality, and more difficult decisions about whom to invite. At times, we considered stopping Meetings Week to save money, but in the end I felt that Meetings Week was a very big net plus for the company, and only occasionally did I curtail them. I believe we took some risks when we invited customers to partake in our week-long three-ring circus, and often we exposed ourselves to potential competitors who were teaming with us at the time. But the idea that SAIC was an open forum of ideas and that employees had a big hand in the running of the company was a far more powerful message than the possible damage that might have been sustained due to the loss of some proprietary data or an uncivil remark.

The development of SAIC Proposal Centers was another companywide initiative that—like Meetings Week—became a turning point for the company. Early on, I saw the great value of having experts perform repeatable functions. In the mid-1980s, SAIC wrote perhaps one thousand proposals a year (when I left the company in 2004, it was writing at least 10 times that number each year). Writing proposals is a defined process requiring specialized skills not always found in the line staff, and it is a process that can be refined and leveraged to gain a competitive edge. Perhaps one of the main reasons that SAIC was able to achieve a proposal win rate of 70 percent—unheard of among its industry competitors—was because of SAIC's unique use of corporate Proposal Centers.

Line managers initially resisted the entire concept of a center at corporate having influence over their own domain—winning contracts. The typical line manager presented with this new paradigm of using a corporate proposal system challenged the idea constantly with the following types of questions:

- Are you saying that you can do this better than I can?
- What's this going to cost me?
- How can I control costs?
- What about quality?
- Who's going to do the work?
- How do we work together?

Fortunately, Jim Russell—to whom I assigned the task of creating the first corporate Proposal Center—understood the line managers' perspectives, and had the answers. Says Russell:

> So we had to figure out how to design, set up, run, fund, sell, and measure performance of the new corporate Proposal Center. We outlined the management structure, specialist positions, operational principles and processes, budgets, facilities, and such, and then worked with the line managers to get their buy-in as prospective customers. It was agreed initially that use of the Proposal Center would be at the discretion of the line managers based on their view of its added value and cost.

Russell and his team assembled a staff of SAIC employees for the first Proposal Center and began operations in March 1986. Centers were staffed with talented proposal writers, reviewers, and specialists skilled in summarizing the proposal in graphical and text formats. These specialists were key to the success of the centers. An employee might not be able to market or to write a good proposal, but he or she might be able to check compliance with the proposal requirements and develop proposal outlines 10 times faster than anyone else. The central position in the Proposal Centers was the proposal coordinator. This person took responsibility for maintaining schedules, interacting with drafters, reviewers, and producers of sections and graphics, and moving the drafts and volumes toward final production. Critical to this process was the use of independent gold and red teams of experts to review strategy and drafts.

Integral to the Proposal Centers was the development of a new, automated online data collection and retrieval system—the Proposal Information

Exchange (PIE). PIE was a groundbreaking full-text search system that provided information on the company's project experience and the successful methods that were used to manage projects; control quality and costs; recruit, train, and retain personnel; and apply effective software and system engineering techniques. More importantly, a network of people from across the company committed to provide the information, keep it current, and attest to its accuracy. Committed employees—rallying around our PIE leader, Becky Leimert Holderness—were the key to success. From the beginning, PIE helped us control proposal costs and win hundreds, and later thousands, of procurements.

The initial reaction from the field to these innovations was, at best, serious skepticism. Why? Because managers had to use their own overhead dollars to pay for Proposal Center services, which were provided as part of a cost center. For smaller divisions, those resources were in high demand and short supply—it often meant a manager would not be able to support a key staff member if resources were spent on proposal support. What changed their minds? A proposal written with the Center's support had a higher probability of winning. Moreover, divisions found they could pursue larger bids and grow faster with expert Proposal Center support. Winning is the best evidence of value, and the Proposal Centers increased SAIC's probability of winning—making them a vital corporate asset.

Another initiative, ISSAIC (pronounced eye-zik), was created to facilitate companywide communication and knowledge sharing. This intranet contains information and tools for SAIC employees including the latest company news, an employee directory, access to a library of forms and documentation, travel information, the time-recording system, and approximately 300 sites on SAIC organizations, tasks, or key topics.

Today, ISSAIC is the primary vehicle for corporate communications. ISSAIC supports critical business needs and employee tasks ranging from daily time recording to biannual ethics training. Responsibility for ISSAIC is distributed among many SAIC departments and organizations. Contributors receive guidance and training through documented standards, guidelines, and procedures. ISSAIC has become a key information source and the focal point for access to applications and tools for SAIC's diverse and geographically distributed employee population. This thought is seconded by Gael Tarleton:

> As for communications channels, what I always remember telling employees is that they had to decide *where* to tune in—there were so many channels that there would be at least one that was right for everyone. The

majority of employees didn't attend Meetings Week, and so they didn't seem to perceive that as communication with them. ISSAIC was the breakthrough in so many ways—it changed the way the divisions where I worked did our business of marketing, writing proposals, finding out what contracts the company was winning (and losing), and it exponentially expanded my access to SAIC's experts on every conceivable topic. It was communication with content.[1]

Each of these corporatewide initiatives was a turning point in SAIC's development and growth—together, they were remarkably powerful tools that provided the inward pull on the many different elements of our loose organization. They helped us build a uniquely fast, flexible, and entrepreneurial organization that had many advantages over the competition. This was proven time and time again as SAIC won contract after contract.

4

The Mission: From Science to Solutions

SAIC is a company for professional people who want to perform superior scientific and technical work, who are willing to work hard to do it, who want to have a say in the policies and management of the company and feel that the company is their company, who want to be exposed to a minimal number of distracting outside influences and pressures, and who want to be fairly rewarded for doing good work both from a recognition standpoint and from a financial standpoint.

—from *Principles and Practices of SAIC*

From its very first days, SAIC was proudly and unreservedly a science- and technology-based business—using science to solve customer problems and the scientific method to create a new kind of technology company. Perhaps SAIC's technology focus should be no surprise for a company founded by a nuclear physicist, initially staffed by fellow physicists and scientists. Technical people played a major and ongoing role in running SAIC, and it is a characteristic that distinguished the company from much of its competition.

In 1968, when I outlined a business plan for the new company—entitled, simply, "Things to do"—at the very top of the list was "Pick a name

41

and letterhead." Some of the names that my initial group of associates and I considered before settling on Science Applications, Inc., reflect the scientific focus of our company-to-be: Rutherford Research Corporation (my personal favorite, named after Nobel Prize-winning physicist Ernest Rutherford, who first described the atom as having a central positive nucleus surrounded by negative orbiting electrons), San Diego Research Associates, Trinity Research, Trigon, Arcturus, Prometheus Research, and Kepler.

In line with these high-tech-inspired prospective company names, the stated purpose of the company in my handwritten 1968 organization plan was simply, "To perform research in a productive environment." As it turned out, no one—including myself—could have anticipated at the time just how productive that environment would turn out to be or could have foreseen the rapid growth SAIC would undergo as it sharply focused on doing important science and technology work for its customers.

A LONG-TERM DEDICATION TO SCIENCE, NATIONAL SECURITY, AND THE NATIONAL INTEREST

Government contracts have always comprised a significant portion of the company's business. Today, the majority of SAIC's total annual contract revenues are derived from its work for the government, including the DOD and the uniformed services (e.g., U.S. Army, Navy, Air Force); Federal Bureau of Investigation; Department of Homeland Security; Department of Energy; Bureau of Alcohol, Tobacco, Firearms, and Explosives; National Meteorological and Hydrological Services; National Institutes of Health; and many others.

This focus was the result of our conscious decision to sell to the strengths of SAIC's early employee team. The company's initial strengths were in the areas of nuclear weapons effects, systems analysis, and national security programs. The key to gaining contracts was offering more specific technical knowledge than the competition at a competitive price, the solid reputation gained through the expertise of our scientists and researchers, and key relationships with the customer who would listen to our ideas long enough to give SAIC scientists the chance to sell their work.

The company's focus on pursuing work that is important to the nation is very much a part of my own decision to create a culture of freedom within the company. When given the choice, people want to do work that really matters—it gives them pride and a sense of time well spent. For many of SAIC's employees, working on vital federal government projects provided them with a feeling of satisfaction that could be equaled nowhere else. The lead technology experts carried as much status as the most senior managers.

According to Steve Rizzi, SAIC's customers turned to the company in times of need—because the company's science was literally their solution. Recounting one especially vivid example, Rizzi says:

> I can remember right after 9/11 how the deputy director of a major U.S. intelligence agency called senior SAIC management to let them know that they needed my staff to do the impossible: scale a system up 500 percent in two days—and the call came on a Friday afternoon at 4:00 P.M. We pulled out all the stops, and SAIC made the commitment to spend more than $2 million in hardware with no contract in hand—just a promise from a customer, a whole lot of patriotism, and a belief in our technology. With the help of some key vendors, we did it.

We reached a crossroads soon after the company was founded: should we push SAIC in the hardware direction, or should we grow as a software and research studies company? We chose the latter since it required the least amount of capital to finance. And we chose to focus on federal government business, but not to the exclusion of commercial business such as telecommunications.

PUTTING "FROM SCIENCE TO SOLUTIONS" INTO PRACTICE

I enjoyed applying the scientific method to business. I saw SAIC as a particularly large, complex, and long-term experiment, where I could try different combinations of people and projects to find new avenues of success. If we had a small success with one particular set of conditions, then I could try to replicate it elsewhere, or scale it up by bringing in additional funding. After each experiment, we learned something new and valuable that could be applied to future experiments.

It's one thing to say that a company is dedicated to turning science into solutions. It's another thing altogether to actually do what you say. Science, engineering, and technology were fundamental strengths of our young, fast-growing company, and the company's focus on these strengths set it apart from the competition.

"Science to solutions" was more than just a pithy slogan for the company, it was absolutely critical to the company's growth and ultimate success. I don't know of any other company that has the combination of technical skill sets as broad or deep as we did. In the early days, it set us apart from similar companies. Later, as we started to capture larger information technology (IT) or systems-related jobs, the pure science-only research contracts became a smaller percentage of our work. At the same time, the software and integration activities became our major activity.

Every company needs something to differentiate itself from the competition. We didn't want to look exactly like our competitors because—if we did—then the only way we could compete was on price. When a company finds itself competing on price instead of the value that its provides to customers, then a profitable business model can quickly become a losing one.

We became good at sticking to what we did best. We had a simple model— sell professional technical services. It was easy for us to change from one customer to another simply by varying the kind of technical people we applied to the project. Many companies are confused about exactly what they are best at doing. If a company makes widgets, and it decides to do consulting in an entirely different area, then its business will often suffer as assets and focus are drained away from the core business. That was rarely a problem at SAIC. We knew we were a technology company, and we played to our strengths.

Since we put organizational experimentation at a premium (more about that later in the book), there were more than a few stumbles along the way. Moving into a project area that was not part of SAIC's core expertise in science and technology occasionally opened the door to some ventures that did not work out as well as we hoped. This was the case with one of our first major efforts at developing and selling hardware, which didn't become a significant money maker until very recently.

TESTING THE COMMERCIAL WATERS

SAIC got involved in commercial hardware very early in its history with the adenosine triphosphate (ATP) photometer. This device detected biological material in liquids from the luminescence produced. It happened in a way that was very characteristic of our approach to getting into other commercial ventures. SAIC physicist Jim Palmer took an interest in it and spent the time and effort to try to build the business. This was happening without much encouragement from me or anyone else. In fact, it was probably with some discouragement because it can be a long, hard path to get a commercial business going. But since it was going to happen anyway, it required a plan outlining the work we would and wouldn't do. That plan would usually be pretty informal.

Hardened electronics—plasma panels built by SAI Technology (SAIT)—were the next commercial product for SAIC. It was a hands-on construction job. We needed special facilities to build the plasma panels because they had to be hardened and able to take shock. The commercial world was a different culture, and we had some trouble adjusting to it. Roger Garrett, who we brought in from Magnavox in 1986 to run SAIT, explains some of these challenges:

> Product sales, especially for a company like SAIC that isn't in the product business, is a tough business to get going and sustain and be profitable. The SAIC strategy of low capital, quick response, brainwaves instead of product is not very capital intensive, where products are capital intensive. And so the question at SAIT was always: Is it smart to be in a product business or not? There were things that nobody thought about, like obsolete material. Oh my gosh, if you've got materials you can't use, you've got to write them off or you are going to get yourself into trouble.

But while SAIT struggled for years, this changed when the company decided to go after a major program—the Lightweight Computer Unit (LCU)—a ruggedized laptop for the U.S. Army that looked like a lunchbox. Because of its previous product work, SAIT had a very competent technical team that contributed to winning the LCU contract. As it turned out, the LCU contract was a success and very profitable for the company, and SAIT went on to pitch its ruggedized equipment to commercial customers such as the automotive, banking, and oil industries (with little success), and to the military services (with much greater success). Eventually, we decided that SAIT was not generating the return that we needed to keep it viable, so in 1997, SAIT was sold to Litton Industries. It was later resold to former SAIC manager Bob Chikowski.

These early programs provided SAIC's momentum into larger commercial programs with Southern California Edison and British Petroleum (BP). Our acquisition of Network Solutions (Internet domain name registrar) and Bellcore (telecommunications software and technology business primarily supporting the Regional Bell Operating Companies) turned us into a significant player in the commercial business world, but we had to learn these businesses fast just to keep up with the new markets.

One of our key strengths was hiring the leading experts in a particular area and merging their expertise with customer knowledge to create a high-tech solution like no other. Another key SAIC strength, however, was finding cross-domain applications for these solutions. For example, the company's work on sensors and sensor networks, port and border security, image processing, and the gamma ray-based Vehicle and Cargo Inspection System (VACIS) all have some key technical elements in common. The algorithms for image enhancement in VACIS, and for signal processing to extract signal from noise—as used in anti-submarine warfare (ASW) acoustic networks—are similar. Some of SAIC's space and laser imaging programs have relied on related mathematical formulations used for signal processing.

SAIC's Integrated Container Inspection System (ICIS)—used to inspect shipping containers that pass through certain terminals at the Port of Hong Kong—is an example of how the company's scientists and engineers put together a successful product by marrying a number of SAIC's technologies across domains. ICIS is a Web-based, integrated security system for port operations that couples data from several classes of sensors, VACIS, radiation portals, video, optical character recognition readers, and more, and performs data fusion—producing a complete data file that can be distributed worldwide in near real time for each container that goes through the port. This is similar in concept to other integrated, asynchronous data networks, and ICIS—which can detect contraband, narcotics, humans, and weapons without slowing down port traffic—demonstrates SAIC's ability to integrate a variety of existing and proven technologies into systems that are new and useful.

LEVERAGING COMMERCIAL APPLICATIONS FROM GOVERNMENT-FUNDED SOLUTIONS

SAIC leveraged its government-funded knowledge and solutions to seed commercial applications and contracts that the company would not have otherwise pursued. Key advantages accrued to the company by following that path.

First, many commercial customers preferred companies with a proven track record on government programs—it helped ensure success. Second, SAIC was able to take advantage of cross-domain applications of its technology. This was the case when the company pulled together a variety of technologies to create ICIS.

Some of the commercial applications of SAIC's technology include:

- SAIC successfully adapted hydrodynamic computer codes developed for the U.S. Navy to a sailing competition when the company helped Dennis Conner's team Stars & Stripes win the America's Cup back from Australia in 1987.

- In the early 1990s, SAIC was instrumental in reducing BP's exploration and production information technology operating costs by more than 40 percent over the first three years of an outsourcing engagement. Since then, BP has continued to realize a 10 percent cost reduction year after year—leading to hundreds of millions of dollars of savings. SAIC went on to work on the development of the highly immersive visualization environment (HIVE) that has contributed far-reaching improvements in how the upstream oil industry finds and produces oil. SAIC was involved in development of the next generation oil field with three supermajor oil companies: Shell, Chevron-Texaco, and BP.

- SAIC integrated a global positioning system (GPS) tracking and wireless communications system to help BellSouth improve the performance of its installation and maintenance workforce, including a fleet of 14,000 vehicles in nine states. The company's browser-based solution allows supervisors to perform real-time GPS tracking and mapping, vehicle status monitoring, and dynamic dispatching.

- SAIC built the Integrated Services Management Center for Southern California Edison—the first of its kind in the utilities industry—to provide end-to-end remote management and operations of all computing and telephony infrastructure. SAIC went on to build similar systems for Entergy and Scottish Power.

- SAIC worked with Conrail to analyze and design a new shipment management system (SMS). The SMS project primarily involves the design of software, database structures, and procedures to support mission-critical freight operations and minimize dependency on existing legacy systems. SMS manages functions required to track the location of trains and cars, schedule and book trains, process alerts, process invoices, and maintain the SMS databases.

EXPANDING OUR CAPABILITIES

To complement our vast technology capability, we needed to establish a systems analysis group led by someone who knew the DOD business. We needed a better understanding of why government sponsors should want our technical research. That someone was Gene Ray who set up a strong systems group in San Diego before establishing our Los Angeles office and leaving to found Titan Corporation. Opportunities were evolving in Washington on military systems analysis, especially related to nuclear weapons effects in Cold War scenarios. Ray expanded into areas of DOD missile system research and nurtured many other bread-and-butter businesses at SAIC.

One of Gene Ray's analyst teams—with a small group of technical weapons effects experts led by John McRary in Huntsville, Alabama—started supporting the Tactical Army missile commands. One thing led to another and these businesses expanded to more and varied contract wins in many areas of the country. The software business started growing as we began adding experts to help there and in systems work. Pockets of capability were developing everywhere, but the best operating systems software developers had origins in the La Jolla, Los Angeles, and Huntsville offices.

Staffing was not much of a problem because the employee ownership, geographical location, flexibility, and market-competitive fringe benefits system were attractive at SAIC. Many small offices with from 1 to 100 people sprung up associated with groups in larger employment centers. Communication was accomplished by the latest techniques available starting with ordinary phone and mail services and ending up with the latest videoconferencing and Internet communications available. Continuing growth was a necessity to compete in the marketplace and provide for our financial well-being.

TURNING POINT: GROWTH OF COMMERCIAL AND INTERNATIONAL WORK

As the Cold War wound down in the late 1980s, leading to the dissolution of the Soviet Union in 1991, the DOD began to look for ways to significantly reduce expenditures. SAIC's management team had long wanted to break into the commercial market to reduce its dependence on sometimes fickle government funding priorities. As federal spending began to tighten, however, this idea gained urgency, and SAIC redoubled its efforts to leverage the good work it had done for the government to find nongovernmental customers. This was something new for us—we were primarily a government contractor—and the idea of breaking into the international and commercial markets in a significant way, while exciting, also made us a little nervous.

The Royal Saudi Naval Forces (RSNF) program, originally awarded in 1979, was SAIC's first large international contract as well as its first large systems integration contract. SAIC began working in Saudi Arabia with the RSNF in December 1980 to study the feasibility of designing and integrating their command, control, and communications (C3) centers. The success of this exploratory program led by Charlie Stringfellow, Bill Delanie, and Dave Heebner contributed to new awards totaling several hundred million dollars to build a turnkey facility for the RSNF.[1] This contract win became a defining moment for SAIC, launching the company's systems integration business and establishing an important customer relationship that remains intact to this day.

The initial phase of the RSNF upgrade involved providing the expertise needed to upgrade their command, control, communications, computer, and intelligence (C4I) program. SAIC engineers currently support RSNF operations at three underground command centers in Riyadh, Jeddah, and Jubail and a system engineering support center in Riyadh.

In the early 1990s, we made a big step into commercial work. SAIC's Cheryl Louie (who joined in 1984 as an operations research analyst developing war gaming models, in the late 1980s moved into line management, and in the early 1990s helped launch the commercial energy business) had a contract in Houston, Texas, to do independent verification and validation (IV&V) of software for NASA's space station program. With this contractual base assured, Cheryl began to look around the Houston area for other opportunities. The oil industry was an obvious target, so Cheryl decided to see if she could tap into it. Coincidentally, in 1992, British Petroleum decided to outsource its IT operations, on which it was spending hundreds of millions of dollars a year to maintain internally.

Says Cheryl:

> BP asked us if we were interested. And quite frankly we weren't—we didn't know anything about outsourcing. But we felt that if we didn't respond, we would be out of the game. So I went before the board and said, 'I've been talking to this company, British Petroleum, and they want us to respond to their outsourcing RFP. The board about slid under the table. "We can't do that," they said. But they didn't say, "Don't do it."

BP sent out an invitation to bid on the company's IT infrastructure outsourcing to 127 companies worldwide. SAIC ultimately submitted a bid—teaming with Sema Group and Syncordia, owned by British Telecom—and we won. The successful bidders were awarded separate contracts to cover BP's exploration and production operations worldwide, and each became party to a global framework agreement that set forth terms and conditions, including which company would be responsible for operations in which countries. SAIC's initial contract in the amount of approximately $20 million per year included IT work in Alaska, Great Britain, and South America.

The initial contract was actually for the classic, SAIC-type of work—value-added problem solving to help BP run its IT operations better and less expensively—on a fully outsourced basis. This work grew into much more value-added work, which ultimately involved optimizing their global networks and providing insights into the next generation of oil field technology. We positioned ourselves as being the people who understood these programs.

Part of the reason BP selected SAIC for this critical work was that the company was looking for partners whose philosophies were congruent with BP's corporate values. SAIC's employee-ownership culture played a significant role in BP's decision. According to Peter Stocks:

> I think we had some advantages as a result of our fantastic heritage of scientific skills in the U.S. part of the company, so we tried to emphasize this background in our U.K. marketing. Translating that into bodies who wanted to come across the Atlantic was not quite as easy. We ended up bringing people over from America, and also developed sources of locally based skills. When I joined the operation here, we had about 200 people

and we were doing about $30 million in annual revenues. We ultimately exceeded $200 million a year with about 1,200 people.

The BP contract built SAIC's reputation as a first-rate competitor in the emerging field of IT outsourcing, acquiring competencies that could be—and were—successfully applied to capture customers in multiple industries and markets, to include oil and gas, utilities, and others.

Both these large programs became significant turning points in SAIC's history. They showed us that transitioning from government-sponsored technology to providing solutions for international and commercial customers could be done, but that there would be bumps in the road. Fortunately, we were able to make our way through the bumps, and international and commercial work became important areas of revenue growth for the company.

5

The Glue: Employee Ownership

Employee ownership is the basic tenet for this organization and probably will continue to be. The basic premise of the SAIC stock policy is that those who contribute to the company should own it and that ownership should be proportional to that contribution and performance as much as possible.

—from *Principles and Practices of SAIC*

Since its founding, SAIC has been a living experiment in employee owner-ship. However, in the very early days, the idea of taking the company public in a few years was in fact suggested as a real possibility. But it didn't take long after the company was founded for me to realize that I would need something special to convince talented scientists and engineers to leave their comfortable jobs and join a risky start-up. In those early days, I was primarily focused on winning contracts and getting SAIC staffed up to per-form on them. As it turned out, giving employees an ownership stake in the company—based on performance—worked like a charm, and the employee roster quickly grew.

My holdings dropped from 100 percent to 10 percent in the first year of the company's existence, and to less than 2 percent by the 1990s. My decision to dilute my ownership of SAIC stock was counter to the typical founder-entrepreneur, who by nature wants to keep majority control of the company until he or she has the opportunity to sell it off. What I found interesting, however, was that the more I diluted my ownership holdings, the faster the company and its stock price grew. I didn't plan for it to happen that way, it just did. Although SAIC's ownership system became much more complex over the years, the central theme of ownership as a reward for performance remained.

THE IMPACT OF OWNERSHIP ON EMPLOYEES AND THEIR ORGANIZATIONS

In 1969, I had a choice to make: keep ownership of SAI privately held, or conduct an initial public offering (IPO) and make our stock widely available. The traditional American venture capital/IPO approach might work best for a hardware company—requiring an initial, sizable investment—but it's usually not very good for a people (talent)-based technology company. This approach is taught almost universally in the best business schools and that's why so many believe it is the best way of building shareholder wealth and liquidity. This philosophy has changed little in the years since I founded SAIC.

We decided to face the ownership issue the fairest way we could—to try to allow the ownership to be assigned on the basis of the sales income generated. In a small company, bringing in contracts is very important. So we came up with a way of making stock ownership available on a sales incentive basis. We began with that approach, thinking to ourselves "We'll come up with something else later on, but the incentive stock award is the best we can do right now."

We started SAIC in the days when the government often awarded sole-source contracts to companies with unique capabilities. These contracts were of course awarded without competitive bidding. I had worked for the government at General Atomic and so had others in the company. We were able to acquire some business on that basis. We were also lucky to find a place to rent in downtown La Jolla at McKellar Plaza for $2.40 per square foot per year. The same space is now far more expensive. We also had a wonderful ocean view that helped us acquire staff.

We were very conscious of the fact that many companies had started in San Diego, but splintered rather rapidly. We were hoping that we could put the stock system together in a way that would prevent this from happening. So we tried vesting and other stock restrictions to tie people into the company. That way, if employees left the company they would have to sell their stock back at the same price they had originally bought it from the company and forego the unvested portion. This approach worked for us—decreasing turnover and increasing our stability and effectiveness as an organization.

I would say that we're going to try to share the rewards in an equitable manner. I would go on to say that it will probably be better than working for a large aerospace company, but it might not be as good as if you are starting your own company and by some stroke of luck became very successful. A number of key people who came into the company thought, "Well, I'm going to make a lot of money on this and I'm going to do it quickly." That didn't really fit with my idea of employee ownership. However, enough people believed in sharing the equity so that the system worked.

When I started to set aside some of my stock to be distributed to current and future employees, there needed to be a procedure for putting this decision into action. We had a special problem because there were few models for us to follow—the educational and business sectors were of little or no help in providing guidance for how we should structure our ownership program. SAIC's local legal staff helped out. On December 18, 1970, the shareholders of SAIC approved the company's first stock option plan, which encouraged ownership of stock "by eligible key employees and to provide incentives for them to put forth maximum efforts for the success of the corporation."[1]

Some scientists and engineers were attracted to SAIC from larger firms because of the environment SAIC offered. This wasn't a get-rich-quick scheme; we planned to share the ownership with all employees. It was a simple scheme, but a new enough concept that some people were not interested. Many, however, were. Ownership went out in small pieces, generally much less than 1 percent of the shares outstanding. It was important to make sure that stock was readily available for valuable employees who entered the company later on. Our stock system evolved over the years and became more complex but more flexible to meet the diverse needs of both the company and its employees.

Many companies view stock dilution as a bothersome issue. Dilution means that a shareholder will experience a reduction of his or her share of the stock value and profits as additional shares are issued to new or exiting employees, or other investors. If, after broadening the stock ownership, the value of the business stays the same, the value of the diluted shareholder's investment will decline. However, if dilution results in greater business capabilities and investments, and the total company grows at a faster rate, the resulting business success would raise the overall value of everyone's ownership stake, including the diluted shareholder.

My focus was never on the percentage of the pie that I owned as the founder of SAIC. I was interested in how employee ownership could be used to better serve our customers and to work for the employees. Growing the value of the entire pie for everyone rather than maintaining my share was most important to me.

There are a multitude of approaches, and each start-up company needs to evolve their own solution. Our approach to dilution was that employees bringing in more contracts earned more stock, improving their equity position. We were careful about how much stock we assigned to bring in each contract so as to minimize dilution. Much of the reason my personal stock holdings were so low was that we allowed stockholder dilution to occur. I don't adhere to the business philosophy of no dilution because I believe that substantially more value can be created through sharing the ownership with contributors and, after all, how much money can you spend in a lifetime?

Ask most any SAIC employee, past or present, and he or she will likely tell you that employee ownership has played a key role in his or her job performance and interactions with others both in and outside of the company. John Glancy believes that owning even just a small piece of the company can be effective. Says Glancy:

> Employee ownership was very important to me because giving a person one share of stock made them 100 percent different than they were if they didn't have any stock. With stock, they felt like they were involved and an owner. They tended to keep a close eye on their own performance, and the performance of other workers in their division. If you had a nonperformer

in your division, the division manager didn't have to figure it out himself—
everyone told him. Employee ownership created a culture where everyone
was focused on being efficient, productive, and not wasteful. We all knew
that if you weren't performing, you weren't just hurting the company—you
were hurting yourself.

This thought is echoed by Chuck Spofford, who points out that employee owners have a different relationship with their company than do regular employees with no ownership stake. Says Spofford:

> I have no doubt that employee ownership played a role in enhancing our
> performance. As employee owners, we had the right—but more impor-
> tantly, the responsibility—to make the company go. In my hiring experi-
> ences, I always emphasized that employee owners really felt that they
> were empowered to fix things if they were broken. Because we had so
> much of our future tied up in the company stock, we took that responsi-
> bility quite seriously.[2]

Many companies talk about delivering quality products, and may successfully achieve this goal, but the public stock markets don't always value
this performance or reward it. The emphasis is on short-term profitability,
and most often represents a drain of resources that would normally be devoted to delivering quality products and services without the pressures of
satisfying the more fickle and unpredictable market.

I have found that employees are more patient investors than the public. They are willing to wait longer for returns because they want a good
place to work. They allow the company to invest in long-term growth
and not just short-term gains, which don't necessarily provide a strong
foundation on which to build. Employee ownership provides an environment where companies can put greater attention on what they deliver to
their customers.

That was one of our top objectives in creating an employee-owned company. We hoped that we would be unencumbered and free to do
the best job possible for our customers. Otherwise, we felt our efforts internally would probably be focused not on delivering the best product, but on
goals such as enriching uninvolved stockholders. Former SAIC board member Admiral Bobby Inman (who served as director of the National Security
Agency and deputy director of the Central Intelligence Agency) says:

I went on the board in September 1982. Early on, I heard criticism from the Naval Materiel Chief about the quality of an SAIC research project being performed for the submarine force. I took it to Bob Beyster, and he said, "Fine—we'll redo it at our expense," without concern about whether there were valid problems or not. The advantage of not being a public company—of not having to be focused on the quarterly profits—meant you could instead focus on, as your first objective, the quality of the work you did for your clients. It established a reputation for competence and a willingness, if there was a challenge, to go back and address it. That simply did not exist in competing companies.

I believe that some variant of SAIC's form of employee ownership can be a good corporate framework for those who want to contribute to superior scientific and technical work and be fairly rewarded. There is a growing body of evidence that indicates a link between employee ownership and performance. Research (see bullet points below) shows that a company in which employees think and act like owners creates the potential for numerous synergies to enhance corporate performance. The employees benefit by working in an environment that challenges them, values their opinions and ideas, and rewards them with a piece of the action. The shareholders, including employees, benefit by enjoying the increased returns that this innovative, efficient organization creates. The customers are the real winners, benefiting from the good work of motivated and highly skilled employee owners who help solve critical problems.

A variety of studies show a direct link between employee ownership and performance:

- In a review of employee ownership studies for the National Bureau for Economic Research (NBER), Joseph Blasi and Douglas Kruse of Rutgers University reported that on average companies with significant employee ownership had better economic performance although there are some variations among companies.[3]

- A series of recent studies by NBER's Shared Capitalism project by Blasi and Kruse and Richard Freeman of Harvard University help explain these variations. They reported that employee empowerment, good employment relations, and various other work practices help determine whether employee ownership will succeed or not.

Employees with the right corporate culture and different types of equity and profit sharing will more responsibly monitor fellow employees.[4] A U.S. General Accounting Office study of 110 American firms found that participatively managed, employee-owned companies increased their productivity growth rate by an average of 52 percent per year.[5]

- There is also evidence that employee ownership works best when it does not create excessive risk for workers; namely, when (1) workers are paid fairly, (2) employee ownership is not in lieu of competitive wages, (3) the employer does not push employees in economically insecure situations to buy stock mainly with their own savings, and (4) when employees' overall retirement portfolio is properly diversified.

- A study of 45 employee stock ownership plans (ESOP) and 225 non-ESOP companies conducted by the National Center for Employee Ownership (NCEO) revealed that companies that combine employee ownership with a culture of participative management grow 8 percent to 11 percent faster than those without such plans in place.[6]

This research reinforces my conclusions from SAIC. SAIC conducted its own studies on employee attitudes toward their jobs. As a result, of these studies, the company found that employees who purchased SAIC stock had more favorable attitudes about their jobs, benefits, stock ownership, and their work environment. More specifically, in a 2003 study, over 70 percent of employees with moderate-to-significant holdings of company stock reported that ownership made them less willing to leave SAIC, indicating that stock ownership improved their retention.[7]

So, do employees buy stock because they are more committed, or does buying stock *make* people more committed? I suspect that the answer is "some of both." When employees invest their own money in the company, they become more interested in how the company is performing. Consider the example of a scientist in SAIC's McLean, Virginia, office, who commented that the day he bought stock was "the day I became ten times more conscious of satisfying the customer."

According to former SAIC president Larry Kull (a fellow physicist who joined me at General Atomic and, in 1970, at SAI), the company's employees liked the idea of working to build a company they owned. Says Kull:

Most people at SAI put in more than 40 hours a week, and some of them put in considerably more than that. There are a lot of personal sacrifices; people travel on weekends, people work over weekends. You have to go home and explain to your family why you're doing this. . . . If all your work helps to make the company successful, then you can participate in that success, including growth in the value of the stock that you own. And I think that's important.[8]

At SAIC, employee ownership was much more than a system of financial reward. It was integral to the company's value system—energizing performance, motivating employees, stimulating entrepreneurial behavior, encouraging participation in decision making, increasing productivity, and making the company a formidable competitor. Employee ownership is the one thing that most distinguishes SAIC from other companies.

PATHWAYS TO OWNERSHIP

Today, thousands of U.S. companies share significant levels of broad-based stock ownership with their employees through ESOPs, but not many companies have defined themselves in terms of employee ownership the way SAIC has. A recent General Social Survey of the entire working population in the United States by the National Opinion Research Center at the University of Chicago shows that 36 percent of American workers have some form of employee ownership, stock options, or profit or gain sharing at their place of work. Of that number, 21 percent own company stock and 13 percent hold company stock options. This means that there are many companies around the country experimenting with employee ownership and shared rewards that are interested in how to do it right. Obviously, it is not done right in all cases, as the failure of the worker buyout at United Airlines illustrated.

SAIC spent time and resources making employee ownership work and we weren't afraid to try new programs or approaches that we thought might help us attract and retain talented employees. Sales of stock to new employees—particularly in SAIC's early years—also represented an important source of capital to help finance the company's growth. Says SAIC's Lloyd Burdge:

I believe the fact that our company has been employee owned has been the overriding factor helping individuals decide to come to work for us. There have always been questions from the prospective new employees wanting to know more about "this thing they had heard about the company being employee owned and what it meant to them." I believe it is one of the major ways we have been able to attract the "cream of the crop" of new employees.

Among the earliest stock programs were SAIC's initial and contingent stock offer programs. Initial offers were stock offers unconditionally extended to recruits allowing them to acquire shares on joining the company. Contingent offers were stock offers extended to recruits which allowed them to earn the right to acquire shares on the basis of generating a certain dollar level of new or continuing business for the company within a stated period of time.

Because the primary consideration for offering stock was the ability of the recipient to generate new business for the company, initially not all employees were allowed to acquire equity positions in the company. This approach was flawed because administrative and other employees, although they were not in selling positions, also worked many long hours supporting the efforts of those who were. Soon, management and administrative talents were also considered for stock offers that were extended to existing employees based on their performance. Stock ownership was made available to all employees in 1973 through SAIC's adoption of a qualified stock bonus plan. This plan was converted to an unleveraged ESOP in 1981.[9]

At SAIC, we worked very hard to be sure that a broad group of employees had access to employee ownership without simply having to use their savings as Table 5.1 shows. Figuring out ways to make less risky forms of company-provided employee ownership available to all employees was a significant achievement. According to Charlie Stringfellow, SAIC's program manager of the $450-million-dollar Saudi Navy program, the rewards—both financial and psychological—from stock ownership were very powerful motivators for the company's employees, at every level of the organization. Says Stringfellow:

As an employee with a stake in the successful performance of SAIC projects and contracts and the rewards that came with the successful performance, I chose to put in a little more time if that was what it took to get a job done well. Also, it was why I frequently put in a few more hours in the

TABLE 5.1 SAIC Stock Programs

	Program Goal	Company	Individual
Direct Ownership			
Direct purchase	Broad and performance based		X
Employee stock purchase plan[a]	Broad based		X
First time buyer program[b]	Broad based		X
Option exercise	Broad and performance based		X
Bonus			
Vested	Performance based	X	
Vesting	Performance based	X	
Stock compensation plan[c]	Performance based	X	
Options			
Bonus	Performance based	X	
Contingent grants	Performance based	X	
Options matched to direct purchase	Performance based	X	X
Retirement			
Employee stock ownership program (ESOP)	Broad based	X	
401(k) match	Broad based	X	
401(k) deferral	Broad based		X
401(k) roll over	Broad based		X

[a] Company provided 5 to 15 percent discount on stock.
[b] Company provided options to employees as incentive on their first purchase of SAIC stock.
[c] Awards of restricted stock placed in a rabbi trust that vested over a 7-year schedule

evenings and Saturdays to be sure we accomplished a task on time and well. This same motivation existed with most of the employees with whom I worked. This was the case with the senior managers and engineers and with the technicians, secretaries, and administrative assistants as well. The successful performance that we achieved as a team was well rewarded with the recognition by the customer and through cash and stock performance awards, stock options, the opportunity to buy additional stock, and the company contributions in cash and stock to all of our retirement funds.[10]

In a presentation to SAIC's managers, I outlined the basic principles of the company's stock program in the following way:

- Make the stock an attractive financial investment.
- Make stock holdings reflect an individual's contribution to SAIC.
- Ensure that all employees have an opportunity to participate in ownership.
- Use stock incentives to attract and retain competent and energetic staff.
- Provide incentives for employees (not outsiders) to contribute equity capital for SAIC.
- Tailor stock purchase plans to meet varied employee requirements.
- Provide a way to sell stock and achieve liquidity for the employee-owner.

As SAIC continued to grow, as the business environment evolved toward competitive versus sole-source procurements, and as employee expectations began to change, so did the company's stock systems. Strong corporate growth and increasing numbers of employees required more formalized benefit plans and compensation strategies. This would include stock directly held and in retirement plans. Other forms of employee ownership—such as a 401(k) plan, a qualified employee stock purchase plan (ESPP), and an ESOP—were introduced to complement the direct employee purchases and stock options the company had used from the beginning to ensure that every employee would have the opportunity to buy stock and become an owner. The company's 401(k) was also a key element in providing liquidity in the internal market.

There were many different ways to gain ownership in SAIC, and new ones were devised all the time to solve challenging problems. Such challenges included reducing high turnover among top performers or en-couraging new employees to buy stock and to receive company-provided stock without having to stress their own resources. However, SAIC's stock programs shared certain common characteristics. They were both perfor-mance based (core to my original model for tying stock rewards to perfor-mance) and broad based (recognizing all employees as contributors). In addition, SAIC's stock programs were extremely flexible, allowing the company's management team to fine-tune the system and its impact on employees in response to changed conditions.

Table 5.1 shows a representative sampling of a number of different SAIC stock programs, most of which were in place by 1996, describing the name of the program, the nature of the program and ownership, the stock instrument used, and the source of the stock used in the transaction.

Although we were privately owned—by our employees—that didn't mean that the government regulators had no interest in our stock system. A few years after we started, everyone under the sun wanted to examine our records. At first—when we exceeded 35 stockholders—the State of Califor-nia wanted to have a look. We kept growing and growing, and soon worked our way up to 350 stockholders. And lo and behold, the U.S. Securities and Exchange Commission (SEC) decided our novel approach to employee own-ership was interesting, too. That really got our attention. But we worked closely with the government and were able to reach agreement on how we could continue our employee ownership model.

As mentioned earlier, there were a variety of ways for SAIC's employees to receive stock to build their ownership. If a company is privately held, the stock is not available to the public through the traditional stock exchanges such as the New York Stock Exchange or Nasdaq, so how do you put a price on it, and how do owners sell? You could certainly hire a firm to appraise your stock—and we did—but SAIC was a unique company. And regardless of the price, what about that missing (and key) element—a market in which to buy and sell stock?

For SAIC, the answer was something quite new—Bull, Inc.

In 1973, we started up a wholly owned broker-dealer subsidiary dubbed Bull, Inc., to create a limited market in the stock and help facilitate the transfer of stock from employees who desired to sell SAIC stock to buy-ers. The SEC permitted stock purchasers to be designated by the company, but any shareholder could offer vested stock for sale in the internal market. In this way, the company could be assured that it was arriving at a fair stock price. Employees—who were required to sell their stock back to the company if they terminated employment—had a mechanism for buying and selling stock while remaining with SAIC.

SAIC's Bull Market

To keep the stock in the hands of current employees and to maintain its employee-ownership culture, SAIC stock carried a right of repurchase that gave the company the right to repurchase the stock upon an employee's termination of employment. In the early days, this right was set forth in individual agreements between the SAIC and the stockholder. In 1981, SAIC's articles of incorporation were amended so that this right of repurchase became a part of the company's charter.

Although the SAIC stock increased in value over the years, stockholders initially had no formalized way to access the value of their investment short of leaving the company. To provide liquidity for its stockholders, SAIC established a limited market system that provided a forum for stockholders to sell their shares and for employees and stock plans to purchase shares. These trades were typically held every quarter. This periodic trading activity necessitated the establishment of a wholly owned broker-dealer subsidiary in 1973 that was named Bull, Inc.

While Bull, Inc., did not perform traditional services like real-world brokers, securities laws required that Bull, Inc., be registered with and licensed by the SEC and the National Association of Securities Dealers (NASD). In addition, the Bull, Inc., staff and management were required to hold licenses to perform brokerage services.

In its earliest days, the number of people buying and selling stock through Bull, Inc., was small and easily managed. Even into the early 1990s, the number of trade participants per quarter rarely topped 1,000 despite the steadily increasing number of company employees and stockholders. Trade orders were accumulated between scheduled trade dates. The SAIC board of directors initially set the stock price five weeks in advance of a trade and, as a result, the majority of shareholders who waited until they knew the price at which they would be buying or selling stock had plenty of time to initiate their transaction.

The industry standard "T+5" settlement date meant that the staff had five business days to reconcile the trade activity, obtain company approval to issue or repurchase excess purchase or sale demand, prepare transaction confirmations, and type up checks and stock certificates before getting them in the mail. Over time, stricter industry standards imposed restrictions on how far in advance of a trade date orders could be accepted and how much time Bull, Inc., had posttrade to release checks, transaction confirmations, and stock certificates. In the early 1990s, the NASD restricted Bull, Inc.'s order collection window to three weeks before a scheduled trade date. Shortly thereafter, the industry moved to a T+3 settlement time frame. These changes, coupled with SAIC's growing employee and stockholder base, forced some significant modifications in how its employee ownership and limited market trades were administered.

In the latter part of the 1990s, a significant amount of growth took place within SAIC. This led to increases in SAIC's stock price and, consequently, in trade activity. For example, the total number of trades processed during all of 1995 was equivalent to just one quarter's activity five years later. Average trade participation ranged between 3,500 and 5,000 thereafter, with a few exceptions. In the October 2005 trade, participant statistics peaked at almost 10,750 individuals either buying or selling stock.

Operationally, administration of the trades necessarily changed over the years to accommodate the growing number of stockholders, the complexity and number of other transactions being handled by the SAIC staff that also supported the Bull, Inc. trades, and business objectives that dictated the need to move the trade dates closer to the quarterly stock pricing activities of the SAIC board of directors. Most of these changes involved quarter-to-quarter process improvements and the simple application of more staff. Because of their cyclical nature, staffing up for these activity peaks was a challenge met by training temporary staff to fill specific roles. Prior to the implementation of certain key technical improvements to the system, the Bull, Inc. staff was supplemented by up to 50 temporary employees who assisted with everything from processing several bins worth of mail on a daily basis, to data entry and posttrade mailings.

To better position its employee ownership for future growth, in 1999 SAIC introduced the capability for its stockholders to go "certificateless." This action paved the way for the implementation of a new online order collection software developed specifically to facilitate the electronic collection of purchase and stock sale orders. (Previously, stockholders wishing to sell stock needed to deliver a sufficient number of stock certificates.) With the online order entry system, employees wishing to submit purchase orders online were able to pay for their stock electronically via electronic funds transfer, a mechanism which also supported the option exercise activity performed by tens of thousands of SAIC optionees annually. Stockholders could easily enter all required information to submit a purchase or sell order without the hassle of mailing checks or stock certificates.

The implementation of the online order submission software and related improvements eased the burden of supporting quarterly trades for SAIC's 30,000+ stockholder base and allowed for subsequent changes and improvements in the trade system to be implemented. With some changes to the online functionality, Bull, Inc., was able to accommodate a significant change to its order acceptance process in 2002. Bull, Inc.'s trade software was modified to allow for limit orders (an order to buy or sell a security at a specific price)—thereby keeping the window of opportunity open for people who needed a larger window to submit trade orders while simultaneously accommodating the processing of these orders on a fresh stock price.

Also among these improvements was a decrease in operating costs, which Bull, Inc. was able to pass on to trade participants. Although no transaction commission was ever charged to individuals purchasing stock in the trades, those selling were charged a fee of up to 2 percent of the gross proceeds. As technical improvements allowed, the fee structure was decreased over time and became bifurcated depending on how an order was submitted. Those stockholders who had elected to go certificateless—and who submitted their orders online—enjoyed a $1/2$ percent fee and the capability to change their order right up to the trade deadline. Other sellers were charged a 1 percent fee and were not able to freely change their order, except to cancel it, after the stock price for that trade had been established. The following diagram illustrates how Bull, Inc. worked within SAIC's stock system:

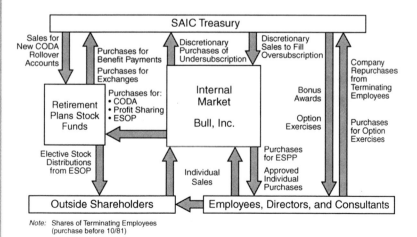

Illustration of SAIC's Internal Stock Market (Early 2000s)

EMPLOYEE OWNERSHIP AS A COMPETITIVE ADVANTAGE

Employee ownership has had a positive impact on those within SAIC, leading to increased employee engagement, lower turnover, and improved performance. But did SAIC's distinctive brand of performance-based employee ownership have an impact outside the company? Did it give the company a competitive advantage in the marketplace? Again, our experience was that it did, in these specific ways:

- *Employee ownership allows a focus on long-term goals.* Employee ownership helped to insulate SAIC from outside shareholders who had no direct ties to the company. Free of the need to meet short-term performance goals dictated by pressures from outside shareholders, the company could establish growth and profitability goals that best suited its own short- and long-term objectives and the interests of patient stockholders.

- *Employee ownership helps attract and retain a superior workforce for decentralized growth.* SAIC enjoyed greater freedom to use stock ownership to maintain a highly decentralized and entrepreneurial corporate culture and to preserve a focus on individual effort and initiative. Being employee owned gave the company greater latitude in designing stock incentive programs geared to a decentralized company. SAIC's equity compensation plans were very diversified and could reach a greater proportion of its employees than virtually any of its competitors.

- *Employee ownership facilitates the alignment of key corporate constituencies.* At SAIC, the roles and interests of owners, employees, and managers were potentially more mutually supportive and overlapping than in traditional corporations that often experience the divide between executive management and the majority workforce with no ownership stake. With employees and subordinates as owners, management perceived an obligation to be more responsive to the needs and concerns of employees. As an employee-owned company, SAIC was better able to respond to its employee shareholders because of its interdependent and self-regulating work environment that placed a priority on open communications, employee participation in decision-making, and greater mutual accountability. This helped the company in numerous ways, from controlling salary levels—and costs in general—to getting employee feedback on important corporate issues, to implementing quality improvement efforts that enhanced not only results to the customer and the corporate bottom line but also the return to employee-shareholders.

• *Employee ownership at SAIC promotes corporate flexibility and adaptability to maintain customer focus.* As a high-tech company in an extremely dynamic and competitive business environment, SAIC had to regularly restructure its operations to respond to changing market needs and opportunities. The company's performance-based ownership incentives encouraged SAIC's employee-owners to maintain a customer-driven focus. The adaptability of SAIC's employee-ownership system has been a key element in the company's success, giving it an advantage over slower-moving competitors.

For years, we said to one another, "There must be other companies around like us. Let's find out how they're handling their stock distribution." What we found was that we were a rarity. There are plenty of employee-owned companies that are owned through their retirement plans. But the vast majority of these companies are not totally or even majority employee owned. There may be only 10 percent or 20 percent of the ownership of these companies in the hands of their employees. We had better relations with our employees and a lower turnover rate as a result of employee ownership, and it made SAIC a more competitive company as a result. We didn't have a complaint-free environment—we probably had more complaints than other companies like us because we encouraged and were willing to listen to them. We didn't throw people out of the room if they complained.

While employee ownership was one key element in SAIC's remarkable rise, and an essential part of the company's culture—giving it a competitive advantage against nonemployee-owned companies—it was not the only one. Employee ownership by itself is not a panacea that will automatically guarantee a company's long-term success. In the chapters that follow, we'll explore a number of other essential elements in our leadership approach that helped fuel SAIC's steady growth.

STOCK PRICING FORMULA

Every quarter, the board of directors established SAIC's stock price using a valuation process that considered a broad range of valuation data and financial information, including the analysis of an independent appraiser.

The valuation process used a stock price formula. This formula was critical because it made it very clear to employee-owners what they needed to do to increase their wealth.

The price formula is as follows:

$$\frac{E}{W} + \frac{5.66MP}{W1} = \text{Stock Price}$$

E = Stockholder's equity
P = Past four quarters segment operating income after-tax
5.66 and M (market factor) create a multiple of earnings
W and W1 are measures of shares outstanding

The price was initially established at a price representing the fair market value (FMV)—the amount at which stock would change hands between a willing buyer and willing seller each having reasonable knowledge of all relevant facts, neither being under any compulsion to act. The primary drivers of this value were (1) profits from continuing business operations (which I believe was best reflected by earnings before interest, taxes, depreciation, and amortization; EBITDA) and (2) market values of similar public companies (which the appraiser analyzed).

In the early days and before we had the formula, the stock was priced at 10 times earnings. In those days, that was a good representative figure in the marketplace.

The fomula was modified over time to better reflect relevant valuation considerations and generate a fair market value. The board first used a valuation formula that took into consideration stockholder equity and earnings per share in establishing the price in 1972. The market factor was added to the formula in 1973 to reflect the broad range of business, financial, and market forces that could affect FMV. In 1976, a 5.66 multiplier was adopted as a constant to better reflect a FMV of the stock. In 1995, the board deleted the limitation that the price not be less than 90 percent of net book value. In 1998, the weighted average shares outstanding (W) was derived from diluted earnings per share rather than primary earnings per share.

The major participants in the stock pricing process included the independent appraiser who conducted a full valuation of SAIC—examining the performance of comparable companies—and provided input to the board and Stock Policy Committee. The Stock Policy Committee of the board recommended a price to the full board of directors during the board meeting, reviewed the price prior to each stock trade to evaluate whether the price continued to reflect FMV, and applied the same valuation process used by the board. The board reviewed all relevant information, reviews, and discussed the recommendation with the Stock Policy Committee, and established the price. This process was disclosed to the SEC, state securities authorities, stockholders, and potential buyers.

SPREADING THE GOSPEL OF EMPLOYEE OWNERSHIP

During the late 1980s, I was convinced that employee ownership would take the world by storm and that we could play a major role. I therefore decided to start a nonprofit organization dedicated to spreading the gospel of employee ownership. The Foundation for Enterprise Development (FED) came into its own in 1986 at a meeting in the House of Representatives Cannon Caucus Room, attended by many members of Congress. For some reason, the FED employee ownership message caught on and the many senators and congressmen attending contributed new ideas. Everybody remembered Russell Long and his role in creating ESOPs. Corey Rosen of the National Center for Employee Ownership and others sat down with us and helped clarify FED's mission, concluding that we were trying to bite off too much. So we narrowed our mission to focus on helping establish employee ownership in high-tech companies.

The words of Margaret Mead provided great inspiration to our small but devoted staff as we sought to promote enterprise development worldwide. She said, "Never doubt that a small group of thoughtful, committed people can change the world. Indeed it is the only thing that ever has."

One of FED's most important early projects in the early 1990s was in Russia. Bill Perry—a future secretary of defense—was on the SAIC board of directors. He had listened to the employee ownership message that we actively discussed in the company, and he felt that it might be good to have us expose some of the former Soviet business leaders to the same message. Boris Yeltsin wanted to transfer ownership of Russian companies to someone other than the government—the employees who worked in them—but the question was, how do you do it? Bill Perry was highly respected by the Russian leadership and they trusted him to help.

Bill became codirector of a new nonprofit think tank at Stanford University—the Center for International Security and Arms Control—which obtained money from the U.S. government to assist the Russians. Stanford hired FED as a subcontractor, and our first assignment was to help privatize the Saratov Aviation Plant, manufacturer of the famous MiG-15 fighter and numerous Yak military aircraft. The plan was that a FED group would go to Russia to try to interest them in employee ownership. What they found was that the Russians had a long history in a command economy and that they didn't know much about stock. Profit was a bad word in this former communist society, and profit and loss statements were unknown. Aleksandr Yermishin, the director general of Saratov, understood the need for change, but his lieutenants were suspicious. The employees were also suspicious of the entire process, and many sold their stock as soon as they could. They knew they didn't want Communism but they weren't ready for capitalism either. We explained to them why it was important to make a profit. It wasn't an easy sell, but Saratov Aviation became one of the first and largest privatized companies in Russia, with widespread ownership of its shares by employees and retirees.

I see FED as a means to broaden the understanding of the power of entrepreneurial employee ownership while helping other companies leverage the important lessons learned by SAIC over many years of trial and error.

In addition to publishing information, hosting conferences and serving as a resource for companies interested in exploring how equity incentives could help them grow their business, FED also worked directly with entrepreneurs, managers, and employees to help design effective equity incentive programs. In addition to start-up companies and small businesses, FED also helped well-established firms implement some of the innovative approaches to employee ownership that SAIC developed over the years.

Although a number of these firms directly competed with SAIC in various markets, I saw the growth of employee ownership among leading U.S. companies as a critical aspect of enhancing U.S. competitiveness. I always encouraged FED to maintain thought leadership by introducing innovative employee ownership techniques to interested companies. FED helped a number of companies that were drawn to SAIC's employee ownership system and that looked to replicate SAIC's success in rewarding knowledge workers with equity. These companies therefore became companies where employees shared in the wealth and helped to create an environment of shared risks, responsibilities, and rewards.

In 2002, the Foundation for Enterprise Development started operating in the United States as the Beyster Institute. In 2004, the Institute joined the Rady School of Management at the University of California, San Diego (UCSD) to foster employee ownership and entrepreneurship through training, education, and consulting. FED has been re-christened to initiate new research and education programs that promote U.S. science and technology, innovation, and free enterprise (shared capitalism and employee ownership).

Turning Point: Telcordia—A Culture Clash

For many years, I was convinced that most employees would jump at the chance to become employee-owners and to enjoy the many benefits that accrue to owners as a result of ownership. This was most definitely the case when we acquired new companies and brought them into the SAIC fold. Given the opportunity to become an owner, who wouldn't choose to do so? As I eventually found out, some employees like the status quo just fine, and trying to transfer SAIC's ownership culture to an acquired company with its own, well-established culture might not be an easy thing to do. Nor, ultimately, a successful thing to do.

Telcordia Technologies, formerly Bell Communications Research, Inc. (Bellcore), is a telecommunications research and development company created on January 1, 1984, as part of the court ruling that broke up the Bell System. Bellcore provided joint research and development, standards setting, and centralized point-of-business process functions for its coowners, the seven Regional Bell Operating Companies (RBOC) that were themselves divested from AT&T.

In 1997, Bellcore was acquired by SAIC—where it became a wholly owned subsidiary—and the company's name was changed to Telcordia. The originators of the interest in Telcordia were SAIC's Peter Elliot and Bobby Inman. George Heilmeyer, who was the head of Bellcore kept asking, "Why isn't SAIC making a bid for Bellcore?" This was mentioned to some of the board members and to me, and we decided to move forward with a bid, even though we thought the probability of success was low. The idea was to use the acquisition to obtain a solid foothold in the telecommunications industry for SAIC—opening up new commercial and international markets and broadening the company's technology base. It had not been easy for SAIC to enter the telecommunications business on its own, and the acquisition of Bellcore offered a golden opportunity to do so.

We decided on the name Telcordia—we thought the name should reflect its origins in the telephone business. But, while putting a new name on the company was a relatively easy step, meshing the cultures of Telcordia and SAIC was not. Telcordia didn't fit very well with SAIC, partly because Telcordia's employees were generally accustomed to more of an entitlement culture. Telcordia had very generous benefit plans, much better than SAIC's. They had larger bonus pools and they didn't have much in the way of performance metrics. As a result, employees who really hadn't earned bonuses the same way as at SAIC got larger bonuses than their SAIC counterparts—a situation that used to drive me crazy. I always felt that you shouldn't give people bonuses and retirement plan perks who hadn't directly earned them. SAIC's employees worked hard and yet their bonuses and their perks were lower. This caused problems for SAIC's management as our employees became increasingly aware of this compensation disparity with their Telcordia counterparts.

According to SAIC's Jordan Becker (chief technology officer for SAIC's commercial business unit, who joined SAIC in 2000 from UUNet Technologies, a global Internet company), the companies' respective cultures were defined neither by their markets nor their offerings, but instead by their founding mission, organizational ancestry, and their values. Says Becker, "Telcordia's culture was defined by their heritage as the regional Bell operating companies information and telecom technology provider. Telcordia was very good at solving specific technical problems using disciplined engineering processes, almost to the point of being myopic on the bigger-picture business issues. Also, Telcordia was governed using a top-down management style adopted from the heritage Bell System, where decisions on strategy and direction were deliberate and the individual staff naturally would not stray from their specific domain or area of responsibility."

SAIC's approach was much different—its culture was defined by the recognition of the importance of the individual, working on problems of importance to the nation. SAIC's strength derived from its "big picture" view of complex or large systems, and the program management required to solve the most diverse engineering and technology problems. Unlike Telcordia, SAIC grew up as a decentralized company that would naturally approach the customer through multiple people at different entry points. Where Telcordia naturally presented a traditional, structured interface to its customer, SAIC's culture was fast moving and constantly changing—making the presentation of a unified interface to customers a challenge.

Not only that, but SAIC's penny-pinching, government contracting culture—driven by my own example—was quite different from Telcordia's freer-spending ways. SAIC employee Lloyd Mosemann (who monthly evaluated major wins and losses for lessons learned) recalls his first impressions of

SAIC's newest subsidiary—and the contrast between his frugal employer and Telcordia: "I shall never forget my first visit to Telcordia's 'front office.' At first, I was tremendously impressed with the luxurious and lavish appearance. But then, I said to myself, 'I wonder what Dr. Beyster thought when he saw it?'" As it turned out, I was actually much more concerned that Telcordia's offices were far larger than SAIC's than I was by their appearance.

Mostly because of significant cultural issues, we began thinking of selling Telcordia. Our management team called for a strategic review, led by CEO Ken Dahlberg. Telcordia's management explained the sizable investments they wanted and said that if the business was going to be really successful, we would have to invest significantly more. The logical corollary was that if we didn't make these investments, Telcordia couldn't be successful. This was a real problem for me. By my own standard, I didn't feel this additional investment was necessary. After the meeting, Ken Dahlberg asked, "What do you think we should do with Telcordia?" And we both said at the same time, "Sell it."

In March 2005, Telcordia was sold to Providence Equity Partners and Warburg Pincus, and today SAIC no longer has an ownership interest in the company. Interestingly, Telcordia had been the primary generator of technical papers at SAIC and, in its prime, Telcordia was a top money maker for the company. However, its annual revenues have progressively fallen over the years, along with the general decline in the telecommunications market. Telcordia's annual revenue peaked at about $1.4 billion and has fallen to less than $800 million in recent years.

This entire experience was a turning point for SAIC. First because of the huge size of the acquisition, and the valuable financial contribution it made to our bottom line. However, it was also a turning point because it showed us that SAIC's employee-ownership culture was not automatically transferable to acquired companies—even if the company was a leading technology company like we were. Just because the employees bought the stock didn't mean that they bought the idea and the culture behind it.

6

The System: Participation in Decision Making

A special challenge to an organization as far-flung as SAIC is to achieve the levels of coordination and cooperation needed for efficiency. As SAIC grows and the groups inevitably become more self-reliant, this challenge could become harder to meet. The Management Council, National Security Policy Group, regular gatherings of technical specialists, group meetings, and intergroup support on projects all provide for a healthy interchange of information.

—from *Principles and Practices of SAIC*

R esearch studies show that employee ownership alone is generally not enough to make a significant difference to an organization's bottom line. To impact the bottom line, employee ownership has to be accompanied by something more: participation in decision making.

Many companies in the employee ownership community—including such businesses as furniture manufacturer Herman Miller, Inc., and engineering and construction contractor CH2M HILL—have experienced the payoff that results from combining ownership with participation. We validated that result at SAIC.

THE ROLE OF THE INDIVIDUAL

Employee participation has always been an important part of SAIC's culture. Initially, employees participated in the company informally because of an environment that encouraged people to express their opinions. Eventually, these informal methods were supplemented with more formal structures, gaining expression in the widespread SAIC employee committees (including the Technical Environment Committee, Incentives Committee, Executive Science and Technology Committee, Stock Working Group, Employee Ethics Committee, and more—detailed later in this chapter) that allowed employees at all levels to have a voice inside their company.

The company's employee-owners had another decision-making tool at their disposal: the ability to vote their shares on a variety of questions, such as electing board members. As former SAIC board member John McRary pointed out, "At SAIC, there is a very broad distribution of employee stock ownership and the voting power that goes with it. Here freedom, responsibility, and resources extend to the lowest levels in the company."[1]

In a typical organization, the lines between those who are granted the power to make decisions—and those who are not—are clearly drawn, either implicitly or explicitly. On one hand, there are managers, whose job it is to constantly seek ways to improve systems and procedures and to make the decisions necessary to implement needed changes, and on the other hand there's the employees, whose job it is to follow the direction of an organization's managers.

At SAIC, there was a chain of command, but the lines that separated those who were authorized to make decisions from those who were not were at times blurred. SAIC was not just a big, monolithic corporation with a rigid chain of command that stretched from the bottom to the top, it was a company comprised of hundreds of diverse, small and sometimes large building blocks (called *divisions*)—each of which enjoyed a significant degree of authority and autonomy from the central organization. Just as these businesses enjoyed a large measure of independence in SAIC, so too did the men and women who worked within them. Even as it grew into a diversified, multibillion-dollar corporation, SAIC tried to retain its small business culture and feel.

Sam Smith, a 10-year veteran of the company, was with us during a period of rapid growth. He recalls his words to new hires, which helped prepare them for the unique organization in which they were about to immerse themselves. Says Smith:

I often summarized my view of the SAIC culture with the following anecdote to new hires and potential new hires: "There is good news and bad news about working at SAIC! The bad news is no one tells you what to do. If you come to SAIC with the belief that there is a pat formula for building a business area, then you will be sorely disappointed. No one will take you by the hand and show you how to define a business area, get a contract, and become a profit center. On the other side of the coin the good news is no one tells you what to do. If you have an idea and the drive and desire to turn it into a profitable business, SAIC has the support systems to help make it happen." To me that is why so many entrepreneurs were attracted to SAIC, and became successful in the process.

SAIC managed to balance the formal organizational structures—board of directors, executives, managers, supervisors, and workers—with the less formal but critical organizational style needed in an employee-ownership culture. SAIC never had the institutional belief that only managers had the best ideas and solutions and that only managers were uniquely qualified to make decisions that impacted the company and its customers. Encouragement of innovation and creativity originated at all levels. Ideas, marketing, and execution were more often pushed from the bottom of the organization to the top, rather than from the top to the bottom. As a result, SAIC became a diversified, decentralized, individualistic employee-owned company where employees believed their opinion was important and that they could share in the corporation's successes.

When Clint Kelly joined SAIC in 1988, he could tell that there was something distinctly different about this organization. Says Kelly:

When I joined the company, the thing that impressed me the most was the fact that everybody I ran into felt that they were empowered to go out and try to grow the business. There was no sense that you were hired to do a job that was very rigidly or restrictively designed. You were hired because you were bright and entrepreneurial, and you were encouraged to act that way with a minimum of process and regulations and policies that would limit what you did. You were supposed to have good sense and be capable of exercising good judgment.

When employees are given an ownership stake in the companies for which they work, they begin to pay attention to how the company—and its stock—is performing and what they can do to have a positive influence. But that is just the beginning. When employees are given an ownership stake *and* they are allowed to make decisions that are important to the organization, customers, and themselves, they will begin to *act* like owners. They become more entrepreneurial—devoting more of themselves to their jobs, seeking out ways to cut costs and improve products and services, and pursuing opportunities to grow their companies and make a profit. At SAIC, employees at all levels took to heart the company's constant reminder that "It's your company, too."

Asks SAIC's Chuck Spofford:

> Can people feel empowered without employee ownership? The answer is "yes," but only with spectacular leadership that is difficult to maintain over a long period of time—especially in the face of bottom-line, short-term investors. Cheerleading only works for so long. Does employee ownership guarantee these successes? Certainly not. It lays the groundwork for sustained success if the initial owners are willing to take the risk with their investment and share the power. There are many alleged employee-owned companies where only the stock is shared and not the responsibility. Those who take the leap by empowering their employee-owners will have a better chance of success.

In the beginning, SAIC depended primarily on the individual to solve problems, and each individual was rewarded on his or her merits. Later, although teams of individuals were quite often called on to address the company's major problems, to be successful these teams needed to be led by strong, dedicated individuals. Throughout our history, we have counted on the individual to be responsible for solving problems or directing a group to solve it.

THE ROLE OF MANAGERS: LEADING BY PARTICIPATION

Growth was a big driver in SAIC. Resources were distributed to all levels of management to grow the company—an unconventional approach practiced by few of SAIC's competitors. But while the process fit an employee-owned company, it had its drawbacks. To gather the resources to respond to large procurements, resources by necessity often came from many sources within SAIC, a difficult but not impossible coordination job for the managers involved.

Managers made decisions—that was their job—but they also created an environment and culture conducive to engaging employees at all levels in the decision-making process. This unique SAIC culture was one of participative management, where employees were encouraged to engage in the decision-making process by giving their candid suggestions, recommendations, and opinions, and managers were expected to solicit and listen to this employee input and consider it carefully in making decisions that all would ultimately be expected to abide by. Participative management at SAIC meant that everyone's opinion was valued; it did not mean that all employees had to be in agreement for decisions to be made by the company's managers.

The form of management for SAIC was traditional in many respects, and the company was managed somewhat like many other American companies. It was (and is today) a profit-making Delaware corporation with a line management structure. It had a corporate organization consisting of groups, divisions within the groups, and a support administration. The structure and organizational culture, however, were more decentralized and horizontal than most.

Superimposed on this line structure in SAIC were vehicles that evolved over the years and that gave employees the opportunity to participate in management decisions. There are aspects of this approach that are not to be found in a company that is not employee owned. An employee-owned company without the vehicles for employees to impact the decision-making process is short-sighted. SAIC tried in every way possible to provide those vehicles.

Our belief (and experience) was that participative management could be made to work with the involvement of employees. These employees had to be enthusiastic, interested in the topic, thinkers, and willing to put the company's interests above their own. By and large, SAIC's brand of participative management worked.

According to Kay Johnson (former corporate vice president and operations manager for SAIC's Aeronautical Systems Operation in Dayton, Ohio), the decentralized authority that invited widespread employee participation was key to the company's success. Says Johnson:

> SAIC granted decentralized authority and empowerment of people within a culture of ownership that promoted common goals/objectives and social trust. This trust became the bond between SAIC'ers that facilitated interaction, empowered individual creativity, and merited collective action. Decentralized authority—within this cultural and business context—enabled

expanded business development and intensified customer focus, provided for organizational and individual recognition and satisfaction, and ensured SAIC's growth and success.[2]

In a rapidly changing world faced with complex issues, informing a large number of employees, debating the issues, and arriving at conclusions was a time-consuming process. It was therefore used most effectively at the policy level, where the line and project managers received their guidance for day-to-day business approaches and decisions. Adding to the complexity of this management decision-making approach is the fact that the solution to most major issues is seldom clear-cut, nor necessarily is there a single "best" solution, and no amount of communication and discussion could clarify the issues beyond a certain point.

"Management by exception" streamlines the process in participatively managed companies. The old saying "if it's not broken, don't fix it" is often suggested as a useful management precept. But this approach—which is generally appropriate for employee-owned companies like SAIC—overlooks the value of preventive maintenance. Preventive maintenance can at times be simple. Passing on ample quantities of verbal and financial recognition (including equity) for work well done is useful, but is best done by the line management structure, not through the participative committee vehicles mentioned earlier in this chapter, because line managers can be held accountable. It is often more difficult to hold a committee or ad hoc employee group accountable.

In addition, broad-based management can be implemented with varying degrees of skill. It's all too easy for endless meetings of large committees to occur with no clear-cut decision or recommendation to management—except to postpone the decision to another meeting. For this reason, broad-based decision making has sometimes been attacked. This process is often associated with the slow bureaucratic management process practiced in the legislative and executive branches of the U.S. government. However, despite its shortcomings, the participative approach has the overwhelming advantage of ensuring that all possible solutions to a problem have an opportunity to be heard. It is particularly effective with an action-oriented or involved committee chairman who can rapidly draw out ideas and contributions and synthesize the better ideas.

If the broad-based management process does not work efficiently, or in a timely manner (possibly because of severe fundamental disagreement), then management decisions should be forced on key issues using interim or trial approaches. Line managers must jump in to break logjams and keep the process moving.

The need to sense the failure of this process is critical or staff frustration and disillusionment are the result. The larger the organization, the harder this is to sense and the more cumbersome the entire process becomes. Periodic reconstruction of the deliberative bodies or committees is thus essential to bringing in new enthusiasm for the process and to prevent atrophy.

The job of listening and responding intelligently to the options that one can elicit from employees on topics of company interest can be stressful for managers. It takes time, attention, and dedication. Company communications systems are stressed to provide timely information and communication. But employee owners want to be heard, and they want to know that their views are evaluated fairly. Often, the right answer comes from unexpected places.

Employees who are temporarily not as involved or harried can at times think more clearly, objectively, or innovatively and find the best answer. One thing worse than having too much consensus decision making and employee participation is to listen to only a few inner-circle advisors. Yes-men and purveyors of only good news abound in all organizations, while managers must deal with unpleasant, harsh realities much of the time. Insulation from reality as seen from the company's grassroots is not healthy in any company and can lead to disaster.

THE ROLE OF COMMITTEES

Employee-owned companies develop a wide variety of management vehicles over time to encourage employee participation in decision making and to facilitate broad-based management. At SAIC, our widespread use of committees was particularly notable. While not the first—or the last—company to use committees to encourage employees to become actively engaged in their company, SAIC is unique in their proliferation (more than 100, at their peak), the number of employees counted as members, and their major impact on the organization. The charters of these committees often overlapped, and few subjects were considered taboo:

- Board committees (active participation mostly by board members):
  —*Executive Council, Operating Committee, Audit Committee, and others.* (See Chapter 13 for full listing.)

- Management committees (largely management oriented):

—*Management Council* was a quarterly "town meeting" that included all levels of managers companywide. Management Council focused on business development, lessons learned on specific projects, and knowledge sharing about customers and business partners. Operational matters were also discussed, such as how to improve the administration and efficiency of the organization.

—*Incentives Committee* examined the financial incentives for employees in the company, with the goal of facilitating SAIC's employee retention and recruiting programs. Incentives reviewed by this committee included stock options, stock and cash bonuses, and various benefit plans.

—*National Security Policy Group* gave well-recognized people in the company an opportunity to exchange information in national security related topical sessions. These meetings were usually Department of Defense (DOD) classified and often included participation by a sponsor of an ongoing SAIC project to add perspective.

—*Business Acquisition Council* reviewed marketing strategies for specific business opportunities. If the council thought an idea deserved particular attention, SAIC could contribute discretionary funds to help get the initiative off the ground. In addition to topical Business Acquisition Councils, there were also geographical and group Business Acquisition Councils.

—*Division Manager's Forum* convened quarterly—during Meetings Week—and enabled division managers to identify and discuss operational issues that impacted their businesses. Topics addressed in these meetings ranged from exploring systems to speed the collection of accounts receivable to nonmonetary ways to compensate and motivate employees.

—*Corporate Risk Committee* identified potential risks to the company and developed strategies to avoid, mitigate, or manage them in a way that would allow the company to fulfill its mission. Although the Y2K computer problem turned out to be far less of an issue than originally feared by many information technology experts, SAIC's Corporate Risk Committee was at the center of the company's response to the threat, conducting special sessions years in advance of January 1, 2000 to develop and draft strategies and policies to deal with it.

- Open committees (open to wide employee participation):

  —*Technical Environment Committee (TEC)* was a unique group designed to allow nonline management professionals from the technical staff to be informed about the day-to-day issues and challenges in the company and to participate in management decisions by providing employee input. The TEC chair generally attended SAIC board meetings (though not as a voting member) with the responsibility to report relevant information to employees. The committee in turn advised management on any subject and suggested issues to be considered by the board of directors.

  —*Employee Ethics Committee,* staffed by employee volunteers— from secretaries to vice presidents—established the SAIC credo and served as an organization not only to establish the company's ethics policy but also to monitor its implementation. Unresolved ethics issues involving SAIC employee conduct were referred to the Board Ethics Committee for recommended action. The committee tackled a myriad of difficult cases and had direct access to me.

  —*Executive Science and Technology Council*—comprised of the leading nonline management professionals from the technical staff—promoted technical excellence in SAIC by every means possible while providing a dual path of career advancement (both technical and management). Members of this committee were considered to be the company's watchdogs for its overall technical performance and helped in identifying pivotal technologies for future growth.

Committees were established for a variety of different reasons, including exploring or establishing new company salary or paid holiday policies, reviewing bonus programs, doing a better job at proposal planning and reviews, and exploring a new business area or technology. The acquisition of Network Solutions, a key turning point for SAIC, was sparked by an ad-hoc committee—headed by Mike Daniels (who joined SAIC as an executive in 1986, and who from 1995 to 2000 served as chairman of the board of Network Solutions, Inc.)—that was chartered to find new opportunities in computer networking and that found this diamond in the rough.

To get a new committee off the ground, those interested in starting it generally pitched SAIC's executive council or me with the idea, where it would either be approved or vetoed. To be approved, a new committee had to have reasonably broad appeal. Most committees held meetings during SAIC's quarterly Meetings Week, and top managers often attended these committee meetings—sometimes at the invitation of the committee itself, or because of their own interests. Committee recommendations were often actively considered by the management and executive councils, with approvals made (or not made) and funds allocated to put the approved recommendation into motion.

Committees worked together as part of SAIC's hierarchy of representation that provided decision makers with vital ideas and feedback. Every committee did one thing well: it engaged employees in their work, and it allowed them to play a role in making decisions that affected the course of SAIC and, ultimately, the bottom line. For the company's tens of thousands of employees, this made perfect sense.

They were, after all, owners.

Turning Point: Composite Health Care System—Rocketing Past the $1 Billion Mark

The award of Composite Health Care System (CHCS) was a key event in SAIC's history. This contract—the company's first to surpass the $1 billion mark—led to a doubling of SAIC's annual revenues in two years and caught the attention of analysts who tracked the federal government's top systems integration firms.

In the mid-1980s, medical care was being delivered to more than 8 million military personnel and their dependents at over 750 hospitals and clinics without access to computerized databases and information management systems. Every day, thousands of patients were treated without the benefit

"Guess what! We're now a billion-dollar business, give or take a billion."

of even rudimentary electronic records, current results, or adequate scheduling. Long lines, duplicated efforts, and wasted resources were a regular occurrence. Military personnel offices, inundated with dissatisfied patients, released a request for proposals to procure an automated medical information system.

Today, CHCS is the heart of clinical operations at 526 (the total number of bases remaining after 11 years of closures) U.S. Army, Navy, and Air Force hospitals and clinics, worldwide. Over 150,000 providers and support people have been trained in its use. Over 8.5 million beneficiaries depend on it. Customer satisfaction measured in more than 2,000 interviews was over 9 on a scale of 10.

SAIC's Jim Russell had been tracking the DOD's antiquated system—Tri-Service Medical Information System (TRIMIS)—since 1975, 10 years before the CHCS solicitation was released. He was certain that SAIC could successfully bid the program and build a system that would work using the existing Veteran's Administration (VA) system. However, not everyone in the company was convinced. Says Russell:

I called Dr. Beyster and said that I wanted to bid CHCS using the VA's system as the basis. There was considerable opposition to the bid within SAIC due to the risk of winning and actually doing the project. At my Business Acquisition Council briefing, the sharks came out of the water and said the VA solution could never win since it was being rammed down DOD's throat. Nevertheless, after a bloody session, I was given permission to go forward and lead the bid.

In 1986, the DOD initiated a "fly off" (competition among finalists) between four proposed contractor solutions to the problem: three from commercial health care software companies, and one from SAIC. In 1988, SAIC was awarded a $1.01 billion, eight-year contract to design, develop, and implement its solution. SAIC proposed modifying the VA system—Decentralized Health Care Program (DHCP)—to meet DOD requirements for the CHCS, and John Warner soon stepped up to lead the program for SAIC.

At the program inception, SAIC and DOD faced four critical problems. First, DOD had a start-up program management office in Virginia, while SAIC's was in California. Neither was experienced in executing processes defined by DOD's Major Automated Information Systems Review Committee (MAISRC). Second, the government had not fully documented functional or systems requirements baselines or developed an approved concept of operations. Third, the DHCP baseline system and code was incompletely integrated and documented, having been developed in modules at several development sites over a number of years. Fourth, system availability and performance were unpredictable and often unsatisfactory.

SAIC tackled these various challenges:

- SAIC's classic approach—placing an office right beside the client in Falls Church, Virginia—succeeded with the collaborative customer-contractor development of a shared work plan and schedule for MAISRC. In essence, the government and industry partners jointly created a "learning organization" to accommodate evolving system requirements.

- Taking this collaborative process forward, from 1988 to 1992, SAIC, DOD, and the General Accounting Office (GAO) agreed on an integrated program definition and development team to address the serious technical gaps for MAISRC. System design, concept of operations, hardware and software configuration, and overall system architecture requirements for operational deployment in the U.S. Army, Navy, and Air Force were all defined. What was the effect of this kind of collaboration? Worldwide implementation of the new CHCS medical information system was completed two years ahead of schedule.

- This "learning organization" model led to SAIC developing innovative processes to test system performance prior to deployment. Then software and hardware configurations were created to enhance needed performance. These enhancements increased speed of execution by three to five times while reducing system downtime by over 90 percent, meeting critical user needs.

Because of CHCS, SAIC created new ways of integrating systems and domain expertise, and subsequently became an acknowledged market leader in the health care information technology business. Performance on this $1 billion+ program led to a number of spin-off DOD contracts as well as commercial contracts in areas where the company had not previously been viewed as a credible performer.

7

The Organization: Organized for Growth

Growth will be sought by internal expansion, by joint ventures with other manufacturers, and by acquisition of suitable small companies that strengthen both the engineering and production aspects of our manufacturing capability.

—from *Principles and Practices of SAIC*

$\mathbf{S}$AIC faced an important question early in its history: How should the business be structured to encourage, support, and maintain the growth that is necessary for its survival? Do you build an organization that is centralized, with a vertical and rigid chain of command, or do you build an organization that is decentralized—flat, and with a flexible set of reporting relationships? Or do you create a hybrid of the two?

These are crucial questions—the impacts of a company's initial design can reverberate for decades into the future, and the basic structure (not to mention its employees) can be extremely resistant to change once it has been established. That design should be compatible with its operating philosophy as well as the types of markets it hopes to capture.

Ultimately, SAIC decided that the best answer was something in between, with a strong cultural bias toward decentralization in keeping with my deep belief that one of the most important things I could do as the company's leader was to hire talented people who could grow the business, give them the freedom to pursue work they were passionate about, and then get out of their way. Or as the first SAIC controller Pete Jackson put it, "allowing them elbow room and the ability to do their own thing . . . allowing them to become successful."[1]

SAIC'S ORGANIC ORGANIZATIONAL STRUCTURE

SAIC began life in the same city where many of the founding staff and I lived—La Jolla, California—but far from its first few customers, which were located in New Mexico, New York, and Virginia. This situation soon changed, however, as the company grew. At one time, there were more than 500 SAIC offices scattered across the United States and around the world, located with or close to a diverse roster of customers and clients.

This proliferation of offices is a direct result of SAIC's unique philosophy of planning and growth. Instead of making detailed plans for future company growth (see Chapter 8), SAIC relied on its entrepreneurial scientists and engineers to constantly seek out new opportunities and customers and then—if the potential business justified it—start up an office close to the customer. If the manager and his staff were able to win more business, then the office would become a permanent addition to the company's roster. If not, then it could quickly be dissolved if the costs to maintain it were unreasonably high, or the prospects for future business bleak.

An example of where SAIC abandoned a long-term business experiment is the case of SAI Technology (SAIT), mentioned earlier in this book. SAIT was SAIC's first major initiative to get into the hardware business, focusing on the manufacture of mobile computing and flat-panel display products. Unfortunately, SAIT never really found its place in the company— which was more comfortable delivering services than delivering products— and it was sold.

It didn't take long after SAIC was launched for the company's entrepreneurial managers to push their way outside the confines of the company's original La Jolla offices. In August 1970, SAIC's board of directors passed a resolution to register to do business in the Commonwealth of Virginia.

SAIC's first satellite office was soon established by Bill Layson (a former senior vice president, chairman of SAIC's Employee Ethics Committee, and board member) outside of Washington, DC, to perform studies of dust cloud formation from nuclear weapons explosions for the Defense Nuclear Agency and pursue work on space and antiballistic missile systems.

Initially, this new office was staffed with just two people: Bill Layson and a secretary. To attract the talented staff he would need to quickly build the business, Layson negotiated a deal with me: if his new Technology Systems Group could bring in $1 million worth of business within 18 months, all of the office's employees would receive stock options. For a company with total revenues in 1970 of just $243,000, this was a very tall order, but it was one that was ultimately achieved, providing the company with an enormous financial shot in the arm, a budding national reputation, as well as a successful entrepreneurship-based model for building the business that could and would be replicated time and time again by SAIC's employee-owners.

That same year, Gene Ray established an office in the Los Angeles, California, area to support the U.S. Air Force's Space and Missile Systems Organization (SAMSO). The office was very successful, further cementing the viability of SAIC's "franchise" approach to spinning off new, semiautonomous business units in the parent corporation's orbit. A year later, SAIC's office in Huntsville, Alabama—which was itself a spin-off of the Virginia office under the leadership of John McRary—won the largest U.S. contract at the time for independent software verification and validation, supporting the U.S. Army's Safeguard anti-ballistic missile system. More than any other project up to this time, the Huntsville contract—won with the help and assistance of Gene Ray's Systems Group—put the company on the defense contracting community's map as a force to be reckoned with in the government contracting space.[2]

I made sure that SAIC's organizational structure remained extremely fluid and flexible, even as the pressures of growth pushed us to make things more rigid and inflexible. If a new opportunity presented itself, we could immediately respond by trying to fit it into an existing unit. If for some reason that approach didn't work, we could create an entirely new business unit. Similarly, an existing unit could just as quickly be dissolved or folded into another unit if a customer's funding evaporated, or if the customer wanted it to be. As the organization grew, SAIC's hierarchy took on a distinctly flat character—when an organizational unit reached a certain size, it would often be divided in two. These two units would grow, and be divided again—creating new operations and groups in the process.

Every year, world events, technology, customer priorities, and the markets we were in changed. It seemed logical to look at our organizational structure at least on an annual basis as part of the development of our annual operating plans to find better ways to respond and react to the new evolving realities. We always believed that the organization should be tailored to the leadership we had, their expertise, interests, and the contract/customer base they developed.

When key people were added (or at times left), we considered changes to the organization to best accommodate and take advantage of their new talents. Finding ways to reward and promote successful leaders often necessitated splitting up established organizations and taking a top performer who was no longer critical to that specific organization's growth out from under an established leader. This sometimes caused animosity but overall was in the best interest of the company. When moving pieces of business between major organizations (whether groups or sectors), we tried to work trade-offs to balance the impacts to our senior managers as best we could.

According to Jim Idell, who played a key role in planning our yearly reorganizations (discussed in more detail in Chapter 11), we tried to mitigate the impact of these organizational changes whenever possible. Says Idell:

> We preferred evolutionary rather than revolutionary changes that would have left our people feeling whipsawed and too internally focused. We at times experimented with new organizational layers—for example, adding sectors as the business grew and then experimenting with business segments led by key corporate executives above the established sector-group-operation-division hierarchy—but ultimately returned to a flatter, more diversified model.

The prevailing model that emerged at SAIC was one of establishing offices close to customers, giving the local manager the authority to run it on his own—with strict financial guidelines—and then providing limited administrative support from the corporate office. In essence, these business units—for example, Huntsville, Frederick, and Oak Ridge—acted like independent companies, and were loosely tied to the corporation through the financial controls and contractual operations managed at corporate headquarters, and through their relationship with me. We resisted pressure to consolidate into fewer, larger units believing this would blunt both the agility of individual organizations and limit the upward career opportunities for the many talented entrepreneurs that we attracted into the company.

This approach of establishing offices near customers—sometimes in the same city, and even in the same building—offered at minimum three key competitive advantages:

1. SAIC could be more responsive to customer needs than could an office located hundreds or thousands of miles away. For example, at the National Oceanic and Atmospheric Administration (NOAA), for example, SAIC supports the National Data Buoy Center in Stennis, Mississippi—entirely in government-furnished facilities including office space, computing facilities, and instrument and buoy-manufacturing facilities. The customer staff is housed in separate office facilities, less than a mile from SAIC's location. Both are located adjacent to a deepwater port, necessary for buoy deployment, retrieval, and testing.

2. Key technical staff could "live with" customers, getting to know them on a personal and professional basis and becoming trusted, proactive, and valued members of the customer team. For the National Aeronautic and Space Administration (NASA) Langley Research Center, SAIC supports atmospheric sciences research and runs a large atmospheric science data archive and retrieval center (containing petabytes of data) that is located in a NASA facility. SAIC has about 100 employees collocated in offices with the NASA researchers to promote collaborative work.

3. It was easier (and often less expensive) to recruit employees who wanted to stay where they were—say, in Colorado Springs—rather than being forced to move to an established company office in Washington, DC, or San Diego. In Sioux Falls, South Dakota, SAIC supports the U.S. Geological Survey Earth Resources Observations System Data Center (EDC) with over 500 employees who all collocated with a 50-person government staff in a federal facility. EDC holds an extensive collection of visible-spectrum remotely sensed data sets of the Earth's surface, including data from both satellites and aircraft. Sioux Falls is a unique location in the United States and SAIC employees there are primarily Midwesterners who prefer living right where they are.

As many of SAIC's managers would no doubt confirm, I preferred that managers not check with me constantly to get permission to undertake new initiatives. As far as I was concerned, the more time managers could spend communicating with customers—and the less time they had to keep running back to corporate to deal with administrative issues—the better. In reality, the spirit of independence among SAIC's managers was so strong that even the minimal corporate supervision that we exerted over their business units was sometimes resented. Many really preferred almost total independence.

This autonomy made a very attractive place for motivated and talented technical managers to work hard. They had their own profit and loss, were doing important work for clients, and, in essence, ran their own small (and sometimes large) businesses, and they had the ability to share in the company's equity through SAIC's stock ownership system. For many managers, this was heady stuff.

Although managers of SAIC's satellite offices were granted very high levels of independence and autonomy—especially compared to similar businesses—there *were* limits. Their independence was directly related to their capacity to exercise good judgment on behalf of SAIC's best interests. When they crossed the line, they felt the consequences. Says Chuck Nichols (who established the first Employee Ethics Committee, served as SAIC's General Counsel, and was an officer of the company from 1970 to 1992):

> Once you start breaking the envelope of what's acceptable conduct and taking big financial risks that can bet the company, man, it tightens down on you like a vise in a microsecond. Because nobody gets to bet the company. And nobody gets to be irresponsible, no matter who they are.[3]

But there can be no doubt that SAIC's unique entrepreneurial model laid the foundation for the company's fast growth and—ultimately—its success. According to Bill Layson, SAIC's success is a direct result of:

> all these little . . . entrepreneurial businesses which only depend on SAIC as a corporation for a limited range of support. They provide the seeds for growing bigger things and they provide ways of accumulating the talent.[4]

Projects and the organizational units that grew up around them were kept with the people who initiated them as long as possible. If there was an acquisition, very often it would stand alone. The criteria used to determine where a new organization would reside within SAIC was primarily based on the organization's size and its ability to function in an autonomous manner.

SAIC's flat organizational model offered certain advantages, such as allowing the company to have many more officers than a typical company, helping to empower lower-level employees and provide them with improved marketing credentials. There were also disadvantages. For example, finance and contracts support functions often had to be duplicated at lower levels rather than being run strictly out of the corporate office, putting upward pressure on costs. A decentralized organization—with highly autonomous organizational units—also does not lend itself to creating an easily integrated management information system. As a result, SAIC ended up with a large number of different information systems at each of the local offices that were hard to integrate.

Regardless, the positives clearly outweighed the negatives, and SAIC's unique organizational approach created the foundation for its future growth.

ORGANIC GROWTH: LITTLE THINGS BEGET BIG THINGS

For the first two decades or so, most of the company's strong annual revenue increase was by organic growth. In other words, the line organizations expanded their business with existing customers and won additional business with new customers. This was accomplished first by performing well on existing work. We knew we couldn't grow unless we did excellent work and had happy customers.

Then, another step in organic growth was to expose customers to new faces representing different technical disciplines and points of view. This included senior managers above the program manager, contracts, administrative managers for billing and so forth but most importantly technical professionals with diverse skills and disciplines that we kept adding via new hires. We learned quickly that when an expert in that discipline spoke to the customer, a responsive chord was struck and often new work resulted.

We encouraged cross-pollination with our customers. Sometimes those who needed to see a customer were in several different line organizations and this became a management challenge. We encouraged these multiple line units to work together and expose our customers to a wide variety of skills, but sometimes the lead unit resisted or was very slow to move. I tried to get the right balance between orderly control and entrepreneurship, but I admit to allowing or even encouraging multiple units to see the customer when I thought a lead unit wasn't being cooperative or aggressive enough. I considered a bit of internal competition to be healthy and we missed fewer opportunities that way. It was like watching a beehive grow—there was a constant buzz of activity. Although we sometimes du-plicated our efforts, we got a lot of business that way, and we tried not to upset too many customers.

THIS SAIC HIVE WORKED SWELL FOR US

We quickly learned that we had to have domain or agency knowledge and multiple skills and experience in the appropriate management and technical disciplines to win new business. Federal agencies are each quite different, and they don't necessarily think you know their issues. Staff with direct agency experience and domain knowledge of the functional area being addressed are required. Line organizations that tried to market without domain knowledge often failed whereas those with domain knowledge typically succeeded. The health care vertical market is an ex-ample that illustrates methods for developing business that we used throughout SAIC.

In June 1969, we formed our first subsidiary, JRB Associates, to sepa-rate our defense and nondefense work and to provide lower bidding rates for nondefense work. We hired Charlie Fricker from Booz Allen to run the company, and he quickly won major program management support con-tracts with two of the institutes of the National Institutes of Health (NIH); namely, the National Cancer Institute and the National Heart Lung and

Blood Institute. The Cancer Institute was ramping up rapidly under President Nixon's war on cancer and NIH's budget was climbing rapidly from about $200 million to $1 billion a year. We performed well on this work, but after a couple of years it became clear that further growth might be slow. So we hired Mike Higgins to develop new environmental programs using some of the discretionary money generated by the NIH work to enter the environmental market in a big way. Soon, we had the beginnings of our major environmental business area.

We also wanted to expand our programs with the National Cancer Institute into the development of management and scientific information systems needed for each institute's activities.

I asked one of our information systems experts to meet with the systems director at the Cancer Institute to see how we could help. After a meeting, he asked us to work with him. It was agreed that our staff would help on a part-time basis. After helping for several months under our existing program management contract, SAIC was awarded a $300,000 contract for systems work. This was a lot of money in those days, and it was an important seedling for future growth.

We knew it was critical to have people with domain knowledge that could relate peer-to-peer with the NIH customers and help interpret programs and requirements, so we hired John Whiteman, an MD with strong computer skills, and other professionals with health backgrounds. We also hired people with technical skills in such emerging areas as database management systems because we knew the customers would want to begin using them soon. In the span of a year or two, about half a dozen of these database management system packages became available and all our customers wanted to use them. To win business we had to show we knew how to select, develop, and operate these systems. We did that. Moreover, we used operations research methods to evaluate and rank alternative systems solutions for customers so they could see and choose the best fit.

From the Cancer Institute beachhead, we then went on to win half a dozen competitive contracts with other institutes and agencies in the then Department of Health Education and Welfare (HEW; now Department of Health and Human Services). These wins were a result of our focus on the health area, strong project performance, peer domain knowledge and astute hires anticipating emerging technical needs. Our projects for HEW included the National Blood Bank System, the National Health Statistical System, and management information systems for several agencies in HEW.

A CONSTELLATION OF BUSINESSES

Following its pathway of organic growth and development, SAIC developed from one core company with numerous outlying offices into a family of wholly owned subsidiaries, partially owned private companies, and partially owned public companies. Each of these subsidiaries and companies orbited around the SAIC core—relying on their parent company not only for financial and business support but also for an infusion of its entrepreneurial, employee-ownership culture and philosophy.

The SAIC family of companies has been a dynamic, ever-changing constellation of interesting and influential technology businesses. In the company's first decade, there was no long-term plan for the spin-off of subsidiaries or the acquisition of other businesses. As such, the organization was only modified when there was a good reason to do so.

In addition to JRB Associates, we formed La Jolla Research, where much of the early consulting work that we performed for the national labs (and under contracts with JRB Associates) was eventually transferred. In addition to allowing for lower bid rates and less red tape, the need to separate defense from nondefense projects was a big issue with certain customers in the late 1970s, further pushing us to do just that.

In 1973, the company reached a new milestone when it incorporated SAI Comsystems, to "facilitate work in engineering services," but also to bid on and perform lower-rate government work. The bidding flexibility that lower-rate subsidiaries offered the company allowed SAIC to win many contracts that it likely would have missed had it been forced into a rigid model where the company only permitted a single bid rate.

As the company grew beyond a billion dollars in annual revenue, it became increasingly necessary to acquire new businesses to maintain SAIC's goal of 15 percent annual growth. Most of the acquisitions were for services companies doing similar work, however, we also made partial investments and had a variety of such holdings. These subsidiaries allowed us to meet our growth goal, establish an environment for doing research that would be less expensive than the norm, and allow employees to pursue the work they wanted to do.[5] Moreover, they served as financial investments that could potentially be very valuable to the company, as in the case of SAIC's acquisition of Bellcore, later renamed Telcordia. If a subsidiary or acquisition provided less than the expected results, then it could be quickly sold off or dissolved.

The outlying companies orbiting the SAIC core came and went based on the company's needs, and Figure 7.1 shows a snapshot of the company's structure in the early 2000s.

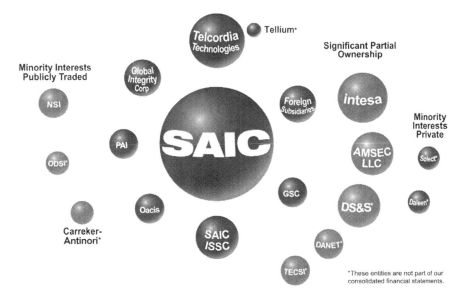

FIGURE 7.1   Wholly Owned Subsidiaries (Early 2000s)

While subsidiaries and acquisitions brought with them the promise of increased revenues and new opportunities, they often also included existing financial, legal, or cultural issues. And sometimes these issues led to conflicts. This should come as no surprise as research indicates that more than half of all mergers and acquisitions fail; that is, they actually reduce shareholder value instead of achieving cost, profit, and revenue benefits.

There are a number of reasons typically cited by experts for the failure of mergers and acquisitions. At the very top of the list is a poor strategic rationale for the merger or acquisition, when a business desires to extend its reach into an entirely new industry or to entirely redefine itself. Other reasons for failure include overpayment for the acquisition, inadequate integration planning, lack of communication, and cultural mismatch between the organizations.[6]

UNOFFICIAL SAIC SPIN-OFFS

Entrepreneurial companies like SAIC have splinters. Talented scientists and engineers decide for a variety of reasons to leave the company and start their own businesses. SAIC had a number of splinter organizations. In some cases, the companies were virtual clones of the SAIC model—incorporating employee ownership, a scientific culture, and more—while others were completely different. In every case, the entrepreneurs who started their own businesses after leaving SAIC took valuable lessons they learned from their experience with the company.

While these unofficial spin-offs didn't make me happy at the time they occurred, I am now proud that many of them carried the SAIC legacy forward. Table 7.1 presents some notable SAIC alumni enterprises, along with the name of the SAIC founder and year founded.

Turning Point: Gene Ray and Titan Corporation

Every company suffers its share of defections—employees hired away by the promise of a better opportunity, better working conditions, or any number of other enticements—and we were no different. From our earliest days, we lost employees to other companies—some competitors and some not. But we also hired many talented people away from very well-established organizations, often using our unique employee-ownership culture as a key inducement.

Gene Ray—employee number 32—was a critical member of SAIC's early technical staff, and he played a significant role in the company's growth. After receiving his doctorate in physics in 1965, he accepted a position with Aerospace Corporation to study nuclear weapons effects. He soon left this job to take a civilian position with the U.S. Air Force Space and Missile Command, where he was put in charge of strategic operations analysis. In 1970, I approached him to join our young but growing company. My apparent powers of persuasion—coupled with the powerful attraction of employee ownership—convinced Ray that setting a new career path was the right decision.

Gene Ray's first work for us was an Air Force contract for nuclear simulation. More contracts followed, and Ray eventually grew his operation to 500 employees. According to Ray, the business model was straightforward: "You found customers; you understood what their problems were, what their issues were, and then you came in with a solution, and you delivered. That's still the way you do it. Hasn't changed."[7]

TABLE 7.1 Companies Formed by SAIC Alumni

1970

1975

Spectron Development Laboratory
Chris Busch & Jim Trolinger, 1975
Acquired by Titan in 1986

Jaycor
Jim Young 1975
Acquired by Titan in 2002

Photon Research Assoc.
Jim Meyers, 1975
Acquired by Raytheon in 2004

DALFI
Roland Fisher, 1976

Biospherical Systems
Rocky Booth, 1977

Horizons Technology
Jim Palmer, 1977
Acquired by Titan in 1998

La Jolla Scientific Co.
George Boron, 1977

Cyber-Comp
Al Ciplickas, 1978

IWG
Larry Gratt, 1979

SPARTA, Inc.
Wayne Winton, 1979

Optimetrics
Bob Meridith, 1979

1980

Science & Engineering Assoc., Inc.
Jim Cramer, 1980
Acquired by Apogen in 2003

Applied Research, Inc.
Harold Jeffreys & Larry Kennedy, 1980
Acquired by SAIC in 1984

Advantech
Lyle Dunbar, 1981
Merged with SPARTA in 1983

Titan Corporation
Gene Ray, 1981
Acquired by L-3 Comm in 2005

San Diego Technical Books
Dan Reifers, 1981

Ariel Systems
A. Mark Hunt, 1982

ECG
Yudi Gupta, 1983

Talaris Systems, Inc.
Cal Burghart, 1983

Hydisk Systems
Bob Hancock, 1984

Chipsoft (Intuit)
Mike Chipman, 1984
Acquired by Intuit in 1993

ROW Sciences
Ralph Williams, 1985

1985

VME Microsystems
International Corporation (VMIC)
Carroll Williams, 1986

Duralcan USA
Dave Schuster, 1986

Technology-Directory Publications
Bruce Ahern, 1987

Tele-Images
Rick Strobridge, 1988

Seneca Systems
Tom Unger, 1989

Expersoft
Dave Porreca, 1989
Acquired by VERTEL

1990

PM tec
Gary Fillmore, 1991

Bluebird Systems
Bob Mac, 1992
Acquired by Open Text in 2000

Epic Solutions
Daniel Crawford, 1992

Computer Processing
Unlimited, Inc.
Dallas T. Pence, 1992

Corporate & Political
Communications (CPC)
Jack & Barbara Harris, 1992

Space Electronics
Dave Strobel & Bob Czajkowski, 1992
Acquired by Maxwell Technologies in 1999

Electromagnetic Engineering
Services, Inc. (EESI)
John Lavery, 1993

TriTeal
Oran Thomas, 1993

Alternative Energy
Systems Consulting, Inc.
Craig Racine & Richard Sterrett, 1994

Veri-Power Company
Will Childs, 1993

DR Technologies
Lyle Dunbar, 1994

Michael A. Peck
Associates, Inc. (MAPA)
Michael Peck, 1994

Metallic Power
Jeff Colborn, 1995

1995

Pro2Serve
Barry Goss, 1996

Ancore
Tsahi Gozani & Pat Shea, 1997
Acquired by OSI Systems in 2002

JNI Corporation
Terry M. Flanagan, 1997

DefenseWeb
Doug Burke, 1998

Networkcar, Inc.
Chuck Myers, 1999
Acquired by Reynolds & Reynolds in 2002

Integrated Science Solutions, Inc.
Cecelia McCloy, 1999

2000

Lighthouse Technologies
Jeff Van Fleet, 2000

MedUnite
Dave Cox, 2000
Acquired by Proxymed in 2003

Genomic HealthCare, Inc.
Roland Stoughton, 2003

2005

Note: This partial list was compiled using information from SAIC, blog submittals, and casual knowledge.

But just as I had originally felt the pull to create my own business when I was still an employee of General Atomic, so too did Gene Ray. After working for the company for more than a decade, Ray began to feel that his personal goals were increasingly out of sync with those of SAIC. When I decided to split apart the organization he had built, Ray took that as his cue to leave. In 1981, Ray joined forces with former SAIC employee Albert "Ed" Knauf, and former SAIC corporate vice president and Systems Group manager John "Jack" McDougall to start a new company: Titan Systems.

The company quickly picked up contracts, putting together a backlog of more than $500,000 within just a few weeks after it opened for business. Soon, the company was doing work for GTE Sylvania, IBM, TRW, Defense Nuclear Agency, and even had a small consulting contract with SAIC. Titan Systems grew steadily over the years, performing on a wide variety of government and commercial contracts, and eventually acquiring a handful of other unofficial SAIC spin-offs, including Horizons Technology, Inc., and JAYCOR. In 2005, having reached annualized revenues of $2.5 billion, Titan was itself acquired by L-3 Communications, and Gene Ray retired.

While at SAIC, Gene Ray learned valuable lessons that were instrumental in his success with Titan. Says Ray, "I learned how to start a business from scratch, and I learned the key factors that you need to focus on to manage a profitable, growing business. Bob taught us all the importance of timesold, bringing in new business, collecting receivables, and hiring the very best people possible. As I look back, what I learned at SAIC was absolutely key in starting and building Titan. When we would have a difficult problem at Titan, I would often ask myself what Bob would have done, and a few times I called Bob directly to ask that question, and always got a good answer."

Gene Ray's leaving was probably one of the biggest events that ever happened to alter the course of the company. It was inevitable because he was having major policy differences with another key employee which I could not resolve. But I didn't want Gene to leave. If he had stayed, I have a feeling he would have eventually run SAIC, and the history of the company might be very different.

We learned valuable lessons when an important member of our team like Gene Ray left, leaving a large hole in the organization. We learned how continuing the fight and rebuilding the business as quickly as possible is key after losing good people. And we learned that we could survive these near-death experiences.

8

The Plan: No Grand Plan

*The aims of [the strategic planning] process are to understand ourselves
from the viewpoints of both what kind of company we want to be and
what real business constraints we face, to be able to assess our successes
and failures realistically in these terms, and thus to be better able to direct
our human and financial resources toward our long-term goals.*

—from *Principles and Practices of SAIC*

A key obstacle for many entrepreneurs starting their own businesses is the need to develop a business plan. The prevailing wisdom among most nascent entrepreneurs is that one should not take any significant action toward starting their enterprise before developing a detailed, blow-by-blow plan that describes exactly what the business is going to do, who its customers are going to be, what its competitive advantages (and disadvantages) are, where financing will come from, and much more. Many banks and venture capitalists require such a detailed business plan as an integral part of the lending or financing process. If there is no plan, there is no money.

It might reasonably be assumed that the now-$8 billion company called SAIC must have had quite a business plan to get to where it is today. Actually, that was not the case at all.

NO GRAND PLAN

When we started SAIC in 1969, it was a time of transition for San Diego's business environment. The city was moving away from its strong dependence on the aerospace industry and becoming a more diversified economy with some light manufacturing, shipbuilding, tourism, and high-technology research. Many observers wondered what we were going to do as a company and where we were going to go. We really had no idea of the size of the company we were planning to build—we had no plan. We just made basic decisions about what we liked and what we wanted as characteristics for the company. Since we were mostly scientists and engineers, we thought, "Let's work on nationally important technical problems to support ourselves financially." So that was "the plan."

How exactly did we go about building an $8 billion business from scratch? Did we spend days drafting extensive plans, or did we decide on a few fundamentals, try them out, and modify our efforts along the way? During SAIC's first years as a small start-up, the corporate planning process was much more the latter. Our growth and success were predicted by no one to my knowledge, including me. Each year, I heard people— both in and out of the company—tell me, "It's been a great ride—but it will end—SAIC will flatten out." I doubted that perspective then, even though it was no one's long-term objective to build a company as vast as we now see.

My emphasis was on growing the business by trying out different ideas, not by excessive planning. Although this approach would by necessity change as the years went on and the company—and internal demands for resources—grew, this organic approach to growing the young business was simple, straightforward, and effective.

Many observers assumed there was no plan at all. But even a dynamic, entrepreneurial company like SAIC—growing by leaps and bounds— needed some sort of plan, if only to help managers and executives anticipate how much funding would be required to keep their operations afloat in the coming fiscal year.

My four-fold plan (and strategy) was simply this:

1. Recruit smart, inventive people.
2. Give these smart, inventive people wide-ranging autonomy and authority, consistent with prescribed financial restraints.

3. Keep a constant lookout for opportunities, near-term and over the horizon.

4. When a promising opportunity presents itself, unite around it and focus the company's efforts and resources to make it happen.

Notice that this strategy did not focus on specific customers or particular lines of business. At SAIC, there was wide latitude. There were few limits on what projects, customers, or opportunities could be pursued by the company's technical staff, so the company's growth followed a natural path, not prescribed in detail by corporate planners. For example, the company's early focus was on nuclear weapons effects. Soon, however, it was realized that the company needed a systems group to address how the results from its nuclear weapons effects research were being integrated into system designs. This led to the next logical step: establishing a strong software development business. SAIC's approach actually became multifaceted, with inroads into new initiatives in intelligence, the environment, and energy.

One difference between SAIC and its competitors was that early on the majority of new business initiatives originated from deep in the organization and worked their way up, instead of the more common approach where executives or managers identified opportunities and then directed those below them in the organization to carry them out. This grassroots marketing machine offered the company a number of advantages in the marketplace. Says Matt Tobriner (one of Bill Layson's early hires, a key leader and organizer during our multiyear America's Cup campaign, former SAIC executive, and chairman of the Retirement Plans Committee):

> Agility in the marketplace was key to the company's success. The plan was more long range—where do we want to be in a few years—not exactly how are we going to get from A to B in detail each year. So, although we might have a plan that spelled out broad areas of growth and where we were going to focus discretionary resources, if an opportunity came up that looked like it was hot and was going to be a good fit with SAIC, the plan didn't mean a damn thing. You just went out and did it.

Unlike many companies where managers have to encourage their employees to innovate and "think outside the box," SAIC sometimes had the opposite problem. There were so many people with so many good ideas that my challenge was getting them to focus on existing targets rather than new ones. However, the planning process is not what got people to focus on targets. What got people to focus on targets were my favorite financial tools such as corporate "guidelines" (for internal investment) and the "F-factor" performance formula that are both described in detail in Chapter 12.

There *was* a short-term tactical plan, which was focused on building the company. We did that as mentioned before primarily by picking the best technical people in the areas that are going to be important, giving them resources, and creating an environment where they could excel. If they don't excel, then you made a mistake which you have to correct in an appropriate way.

While for many years there was no strategic (long-term) plan for managers to adhere to, there were annual short-term tactical financial plans that did require their utmost attention. Financial plans and the financial planning process at SAIC were very disciplined and systematic—it was the flip side of the expansive freedom that the company's technologists had the privilege of enjoying.

The company's financial plans got their start in the first few years of SAIC's existence, when our business advisor Art Biehl insisted that every serious company needed a plan. This annual financial plan eventually evolved into a system of quarterly, mid-year, end-of-year, and other financial plans and reports—all used to help guide manager's decisions, and to provide a way for their bosses to monitor their progress. Larry Kull integrated an early form of strategic planning together with the existing financial planning efforts—creating a more formal corporate planning function that survived for a number of years after he left SAIC.

Although I never restrained the company's formal planning efforts, as far as I was concerned, SAIC would be better off if our leaders would make the future instead of soul-searching about it. I don't think we ever had a grand plan. However, we did have a plan for how to get from today to the end of the fiscal year. We made quick decisions, moved out, and adjusted the plan as time went on. We began writing strategic plans in the more recent past, many of which ended up in a drawer and few ever read them. We always had one-year plans which we took seriously, and I considered them to be more than just plans—they were commitments.

THE PLANNING PROCESS

The SAIC planning process looked very different than those in most public companies. Because of the inherent unpredictability in an organization that emphasized a culture of entrepreneurship, where employees were granted the freedom and autonomy to pursue customers and projects that most interested them, I had little interest in such plans. They tended to take a lot of time for people to complete and invariably bore little resemblance to what the organization actually experienced. We seemed to be better off with short-term operational plans.

From the earliest days, Larry Kull and others encouraged me to spend some time thinking about strategy and getting my thoughts down in writing. This first round of "strategic thinking" helped me set out some broad objectives and strategy ideas (which were the forerunners to the *Principles and Practices of SAIC* employee handbook), and to get the word around on what kind of company we wanted to be and how we were going to operate.

This appeared to be sufficient for a while, but in the late 1970s with so much going on and the company getting large, I started feeling uncomfortable about whether we were really headed in the right direction. So in the usual SAIC fashion, I got a small group together to meet with me regularly to think about the longer term and set some additional strategy for the company, if that seemed appropriate to us. The group was made up of Jim Foster, Ed Frieman, Tom Hicks, Michael Higgins, Hugh Kendrick, Larry Kull, John McRary, Ed Straker, and Matt Tobriner, with Michael taking the lead in scheduling meetings and shepherding the process along. We met every two months or so for several years.

I called it the Clandestine Strategy Group because we really didn't make much of a fuss about what we were doing or draw up documents detailing what everyone else should do. That's not how I wanted to run the company, and we were pretty sure that the managers we had would probably ignore such a document anyway. But the group helped me in many ways because:

- It forced me to take some time for strategic thinking and record and disseminate my thoughts.
- It helped me develop and continually revise and update *Principles and Practices of SAIC,* the "how" of our approach to doing things.
- It devised the longer-term goals of $1 billion in revenues by the end of FY1990, and the growth rates, profit rates, and stock price growth required to get there—the "what" of our approach.

- It developed the Business Areas and Business Lines approach to tracking and analyzing what the whole company was doing across the board and trying to recognize problems, conflicts, and resource needs before they became crises.

- It helped (with Randy Vosti, a senior financial manager for 20 years at SAIC corporate and sector levels) to coordinate and rationalize the profit centers' annual operating plans and make sure they were consistent with our "strategic thinking," and eventually to develop three-year, fully coordinated financial plans by business line. (By early 1984, we were projecting revenues by business line out through FY1990, showing that it was plausible to reach the $1.05 billion goal for that year; and we achieved that strategic goal right on plan in FY1990.) One characteristic of the strategic plans was we always "made" the revenue and profit plans, but almost never with the business mix we had "planned."

- I recognized early on the need to make a major push into hardware and software systems integration if we expected to make our 20 percent per year revenue growth goal. This evolved into a detailed "Systems Integration Strategic Plan" to guide us.

- It helped me decide how to allocate scarce corporate discretionary resources among the hundreds of competing demands and to steer at least some of those resources into strategic areas.

- It continually analyzed and made recommendations for improving the management information system (MIS) and the proposal management system to make them more useful for companywide planning and management. The business areas approach was key to this.

To complement the Strategic Planning Committee and provide longer-term insight from outside the company, I asked former Defense Secretary Harold Brown to chair a little group of very smart people to work with us. The idea was to help me understand (and pay attention to) what was going on in the world that might impact us in the long term, particularly with regard to technology. The Brown Panel (Harold Brown, John Deutch, Gene Fubini, Henry Rowan, John Toomay, and Jasper Welch) played a key role in the strategic thinking and planning that went on.

The Charter for the New Strategic Planning Committee (1981)

- Provide a forum for addressing strategic issues on a regular basis.
- Develop concepts of what the company is now and how it should develop.
- Define basic markets and types of businesses in which the company intends to operate for the long term.
- Develop general objectives and plans for the company in each major market and business line.
- Draw up a statement of SAIC's broad operating principles, objectives, and strategy.
- Develop more specific objectives and strategy in the following areas:

  —Growth and business mix

  —Capital structure

  —Organizational structure

  —Investment of discretionary resources

  —Acquisitions and divestitures

  —Key personnel acquisition and retention

  —Develop a strategic plan (four to six years ahead), update it periodically, and track the company's progress in meeting it.

By contrast, operational planning was a bottom-up affair, but it was hugely important to me in managing the company. Every year, each line manager prepared a detailed plan for the coming year. These got worked over at successive layers of the organization and eventually got to me where intense negotiations went on to nail down exactly what each profit center manager would commit to. They also told me where they needed help and what new areas they wanted to explore. Each one wanted some resources from corporate to pursue their ideas.

All this took a lot of time, which bothered me, but it was absolutely necessary to get their financial commitments nailed down, coordinated, and supported because I was going to hold each manager strictly accountable to meet his or her plan. Over time, this operational planning got very complicated with quarterly, semiannual, and year-end reports and revisions, and the management information system had a hard time keeping up. But we managed to keep reasonable tabs on what people were doing financially while giving them as much freedom as possible to run their organizations.

The main motivation at SAIC for having the planning process was to ensure that the company would meet its desired targets for stock price growth. If there were gaps in certain areas, then discretionary funds could be directed from the corporate "guideline" pool to shore up those divisions or to pursue new programs. SAIC's fiscal year ran from February 1 through January 31, and planning instructions—including bid rates and other planning guidelines—were sent to the various organizational units at the end of September, giving them October and November to work on their annual plans before corporate reviews began. The plans would be collected in the beginning of December, with inputs consolidated by corporate during the first couple weeks of the month. The last weeks of December were spent in plan review meetings with each of the line organizations. This was the line organizations' opportunity to brief me on their plans—with an emphasis on business development.

The system worked because the company rewarded managers who increased their revenues within certain targets, and managers worked hard to ensure that the minimum targets were met. It also worked because managers were rewarded for *actual* performance—not for the difference between planned and actual performance as managers are at many organizations. There was therefore no benefit in negotiating a conservative plan or in sandbaging results.

This approach resulted in less predictability in the planning process. Being an employee-owned, private company allowed SAIC to tolerate this unpredictability in favor of the possibility of exceeding growth targets. However, the markets in which public companies today operate sometimes value predictability over absolute performance. Public companies today therefore do more top-down planning because the emphasis and priority is on hitting the plan. Variance from the plan—sometimes even a positive one—could have consequences.

In SAIC's early days if we saw an opportunity, we pursued it—often to good result. Such was the case in our approach to entering and building our health care business through JRB Associates. JRB Associates' employees had helped me with consulting at Los Alamos, including the medical program at the Los Alamos Meson Factory. Under Duncan Pruitt and Lynn Colquill, we built a wide-ranging and successful business consulting on medical cancer radiation protocols using an electron linear accelerator and—in later years—proton accelerators for cancer therapy.

Hospitals like M. D. Anderson Cancer Center (Houston) and others commissioned us to help design their radiation-shielded facilities and write their linear accelerator specifications. Many of the key people like Dave Gross and Charlie Fricker helped establish our medical business, and we built up this business rapidly—with little or no advance planning. Most of the accelerators we helped install were funded by the National Cancer Institute (NCI).

The M. D. Anderson Radiation Treatment Center was one of the five largest radiation facilities and hospitals in the nation. This work provided key credibility for us when we bid the NCI planning support contract. We had been working both directly and indirectly with NCI over many years, but mainly in the facility area.

Another source of introductions to major program areas was provided by Mike Dowe, who had joined SAIC to work on DOD programs. He was a specialist in the high-technology Defense Advanced Research Projects Agency (DARPA) beam weapons area. SAIC, at that time, had a $3 million revenue level, and the new NCI prime contract with JRB Associates was also at the $3 million level. Although this was a lot for us to bite off, we kept at it until we eventually succeeded. This contract spawned much more work with NCI and led to our winning a prestigious government-owned contractor-operated (GOCO) prime contract to run the large medical support services area of the NCI and part of the Institute's facility at Edgewood Arsenal.

The NCI support contract was an interesting novelty for us because, according to NCI rules, we had to bid the contract at a very low fee (profit) to be considered for award. There were also some restrictions on our using the NCI contract to attract similar contracts from other potential customers. Although we barely broke even with the contract finances, the GOCO contract allowed us to hire outstanding medical researchers, exposing us to the forefront of cancer medical research and, as it turned out, positioning us for the biotechnology and bioterrorism thrusts that developed in early 2000.

This experience proved that SAIC could run a large, by-the-book contract, choosing our own subcontractors and participating in the selection of senior staff. We did not have a large, complex, multiyear plan for entering into the medical business. We simply had a deep desire to find new business opportunities in this area, and then do all we could to win them. When the opportunity presented itself, we recognized the potential for this line of business and acted quickly. While the medical business eventually became integrated into the more intensive corporate planning process, our initiatives in this area were not as we had experienced in SAIC's early years.

Turning Point: Network Solutions— Launching SAIC into a New Orbit

I can't count the number of times when a manager in one of our many offices decided to go after a new customer or contract, independently acted on it, and as a result built a profitable new business area for the company. I just know there were many. I do remember some memorable occasions, however, and our acquisition of Network Solutions, Inc. stands out in my mind.

In 1993, Herndon, Virginia-based Network Solutions, Inc.—a small, minority-owned 8(a) business—entered into a cooperative agreement with the National Science Foundation (NSF) to develop and run the Internet's domain name registration service—instantly becoming a government-blessed monopoly with the sole power to assign the .com, .org, .net, .edu, and .gov addresses that route users on the Internet. Our story began in 1993, when SAIC's Mike Daniels met with Network Solutions, Inc.'s CEO Emmitt McHenry to discuss a possible acquisition. Says Mike Daniels about these early discussions:

> I talked to Emmitt McHenry in 1993 about a possible acquisition after they won the NSF domain naming agreement, specifically because I had been at ARPA during 1969/1971, when the first-ever funds were put into the ARPANET, which years later became the Internet. I had closely followed the development of the ARPANET and then the Internet all those years— watching it evolve to the possible point of commercialization. In 1994, I presented the first of a series of briefings to Bob Beyster, and then to the board of directors, regarding the possible acquisition.

When SAIC decided in 1995 to acquire Network Solutions, however, it wasn't because of its domain registry business. The main reason was the company's ability to build data networks. But the acquisition would not have happened at all without the persistence of Mike Daniels in making the case for acquiring the company. I sided with Daniels and supported his efforts, and the deal was done.

With $25 million in annual telecommunications consulting revenues, 400 employees located within a stone's throw of SAIC's Northern Virginia offices, and name-brand clients such as NationsBank and AT&T, purchasing Network Solutions made sense for many different reasons. As Network Solutions was being absorbed by its new parent company, SAIC, the Internet domain name registration business was starting to expand—showing potential for rapid growth.

In late 1995, the NSF granted Network Solutions the authority to charge customers a fee to register their domain names. Up until that point, the NSF had subsidized the domain registration service—a practice that inevitably had to change as the number of commercial registrations began to grow and the costs to support them began to climb. Network Solutions—after it became a wholly owned subsidiary of SAIC—established an annual fee of $50 per domain name registered, or $100 for two years. Establishing this new domain name business required the ultimate skill in negotiations with many stakeholders, but the federal government—seeing the potential of this new information technology—helped push this forward.

At about the same time, commercial firms began to discover the vast promise of the Internet, snapping up domain names and establishing new web sites. The boom was on. When SAIC acquired Network Solutions in 1995, there were just over 100,000 domain names. On November 6, 1998, Network Solutions registered its three *millionth* domain name and, only a year later, that number had doubled to more than six million domain names. NSI built the commercial worldwide domain name business in countries throughout the world and soon became a household name—helping to build the tidal wave of global Internet usage by making it easy to use.

We quickly recognized that Network Solutions was the tollbooth on the Information Highway, and that the company had become an extremely valuable asset. In part to determine a realistic valuation for the company, in 1997 we decided to sell 20 percent of Network Solutions through an initial public offering—raising $67 million. A secondary offering in 1999—which reduced SAIC's ownership stake to 45 percent of Network Solutions—raised another $779 million in what was then the largest-ever Internet equity offering. A follow-on offering in early 2000 raised $2.3 billion, the largest Internet offering in history at that time. Finally, in March 2000—at what proved to be the height of the dot-com boom—Network Solutions was sold to Mountain View, California-based VeriSign Corporation for $19.6 *billion* in stock, of which SAIC's remaining stake was $3.4 billion. Considering the $4.5

million acquisition price, this was an excellent return on investment for SAIC's employee shareholders.

This experience reinforced our core value of allowing and encouraging individual entrepreneurs to find and act on opportunities—wherever they might occur. It also showed how tactical thinking in the company and not just top-down planning could launch us into an entirely new orbit. Mike Daniels saw the promise in this small, financially stressed company—Network Solutions—and turned it into something that had major significance for the nation and the world.

9

The Pitch:
Everyone a
Salesperson

*How we go about our marketing is one of the most important
consideration for the future of SAIC. Successful marketing is built
primarily upon the reputation of the company and our technical staff for
performing superior and, in some cases, unique technical work.*

—from *Principles and Practices of SAIC*

When an entrepreneur starts a new business, he or she may wear many hats, including manager, recruiter, designer, bookkeeper, builder, salesperson, quality assurance representative, and more. However, as the entrepreneur begins to hire people to take over these specific tasks, his or her focus usually narrows to doing those essential things that have the greatest potential impact on bringing new business into the company.

At SAIC, selling was very much the job of every technical employee, from managers on down the line. Our philosophy was if you could sell, then you could likely run a division. So long as you were bringing new business into the company, then you would likely be given the opportunity to manage people and the business units that employed them.

SELLING: A
REWARDING OPPORTUNITY

For most of its more than three decades, SAIC did not have a traditional marketing organization. Not only did technical people—scientists, engineers, and others—run the company, they also sold for the company. Each of these employees was charged with the responsibility of bringing business into the company, and it was up to them to decide how best to do that. In essence, the company used a "franchise" model with corporate providing support in the legal, administrative, and financial areas that they had little interest in doing themselves. For managers, this meant that they could design their organization in whatever way they wanted, and pursue almost any technical area or customer that interested them, so long as they didn't consume more overhead than planned.

This "seller-doer" model of marketing put the initial emphasis on hiring people who were in business areas that SAIC knew something about. As the company grew, there were more business areas the company knew about—opening up ever-increasing opportunities for new business. Once the company landed a contract, the emphasis was on performing well, however, marketing wasn't far behind for these talented doers. Matt Tobriner explains that everyone in the company was expected to participate in the selling process in some way, whether directly or indirectly. Says Tobriner:

> Everybody had to learn to become a marketing agent for the company. And if you weren't good at that, as long as you found someone within SAIC who was willing to keep you alive and feed you work, that was fine. A lot of guys were technically oriented people who were very good at what they did in a narrow specialty. Everybody wanted them on their contracts because they could solve tough problems. But even these people were expected to help write proposals and get in front of the customer and represent the company outside the work environment.

Some employees were better than others at selling new work to customers. Some could stand up and do a credible and even impressive sales presentation, while others could not. The people who had a talent for selling were focused on that role. We emphasized technical people in sales roles who could develop and explain in detail how a solution worked and provided real (not an illusion of) benefits. We sought people who wanted to make a genuine impact.

"But its most outstanding feature is that it can create the illusion that work is being done."

Beyond ensuring their ongoing employment by meeting financial objectives, marketing was the most direct way that employees could have a positive impact on the company's financial prospects. SAIC's employee-owners could see the benefits that their sales efforts had on the bottom line and the stock price, which rewarded them for building the equity of SAIC. We had a clear, unambiguous accountability system with metrics tied to the stock price that kept all organizational levels pulling on the same oar. The end game: increase the stock price and thereby benefit every employee-owner. In a publicly traded company, it is challenging to connect personal performance to the stock price. At SAIC, we were constantly reminded that our day-to-day performance had a direct impact on customer satisfaction—the key to profitability and growth.

But the rewards of winning a new contract, opening up a new market, or growing the business weren't just financial. We regularly gave public "attaboy's" to employees who had made a significant contribution to SAIC's success. In addition, line organizations were internally known and regularly referred to by the leader's name (e.g., Straker Sector, Hutchinson Group). This practice didn't just humanize the groups, going beyond SAIC's official but functional organizational unit titles such as the International Sector or the Nuclear Technology Group, it served to further motivate some already very motivated leaders. In addition, most of the company's leadership was seated in a conspicuous place at Meetings Week—these leaders considered it an honor to have a seat "at the table."

Kevin Winstead, director of corporate planning—who joined SAIC as an accountant in 1981—recalls how we harnessed the energy of our motivated managers and directed it to the good of SAIC—and our customers:

> The thing that struck me was how sometimes extraordinary personal ambitions were harnessed and redirected toward company-level goals. Not always, but often. And that was somehow further refracted toward client problems (often national security), which was always acknowledged as important at the top of the company. That acknowledgment from the top created a further acceleration of the momentum. And, eventually, the contributions of administrative functions helped. It just keeps building and building so that one thing begets the next and so on. This snowball just kept rolling down the hill and growing bigger and bigger.[1]

Not everyone talented in doing a specific technical task, or who was a great people manager, was an effective marketer—it took a special person with the right blend of expertise and personality—the "triple-threat" person mentioned earlier in this book. Things changed with time and as we continued to grow. Later, we established business acquisition councils, proposal development centers, and formalized processes for making large bid decisions, critiquing proposals, and developing cost strategies.

SOFTWARE AND SYSTEMS INTEGRATION—SAIC'S BREAD AND BUTTER

SAIC's efforts in systems integration started when we were just a small organization. And the reason for this was that SAIC was so small, it had to integrate its activities together with those of other companies to make a winning bid. We were able to bid contracts like the Department of Defense (DOD) Composite Health Care System (CHCS) contract as the lead (prime) bidder. But in the case of many contracts of interest, we needed a systems integration partner. We would have to accept a smaller role just to partner in these contracts. That process, however, allowed us to compete and win against well-established companies like Lockheed Martin and Northrop. They would normally prime bids, and we would sometimes be their subcontractor if it looked like they were going to win. So, often, we didn't prime. We had many advantages that we could leverage, such as special expertise and lower bid rates that the big guys couldn't easily compete with.

The Saudi systems integration contract came along early in our history. SAIC Comsystems contracts were all systems integration contracts. Comsystems was primarily working in San Diego for the naval commands at Naval Ocean Systems Center (NOSC) and Space and Naval Warfare Systems Command (SPAWAR) on command and control systems like the Worldwide Military Command and Control System (WWMCCS). We hired the people from our local competitors like Computer Sciences Corporation (CSC) to go after this business. The Electric Power Research Institute (EPRI) in Palo Alto, California, brought us into nuclear reactor safety, developing the statistical methodology for assessing the probability of certain kinds of serious risk (reactor core meltdown, for example). We were jointly trying to come up with a way to make nuclear reactor systems less vulnerable to component or human failure.

SAIC's first major software development and independent verification and validation (IV&V) job was for the U.S. Army Missile Command in Huntsville, Alabama. John McRary—our regional representative—pieced together capabilities from throughout SAIC and our bidding partners. Early on, in 1978, we also had a big systems integration contract with the Bureau of Land Management (BLM) in Washington, DC, completing biological sampling in the Southern California Bight region of the Pacific Ocean. The program went on for many years until all the baseline biological sampling was accomplished for BLM.

Hardened electronics projects started in 1981. Flight simulation programs began on the Patriot missile in 1982 under the Huntsville Missile Command program. We would very often hire many of the staff members who had retired from these agencies because they were known and were trusted by our customers and had strong capabilities. We also continued to staff from La Jolla when technical specialties were needed. The problem was that the La Jolla people were quite expensive compared with expected reimbursement rates in Huntsville. We had to find ways to work with the customer to reduce costs by hiring people there. This strategy was very effective.

Wayne Winton was one such individual who joined SAIC after leaving Missile Command. He later left SAIC and started Sparta, Inc. He wanted to do his own thing and became very successful at it. His stock ownership system was patterned after SAIC's. I always liked and respected him, and we have maintained an amicable arrangement over the years. He would bid against us at times, but he would also bid with us at times. Between us, we had an unspoken agreement that we would try to work together.

Wayne Winton did very well in Huntsville, where SAIC had had a more difficult time. Eventually, John McRary (the group manager) hired his own people, mostly local and well known in Huntsville. Our business was focused primarily on analysis for the Patriot missile program, including warhead vulnerability. Our research staff was good at reentry physics, so we helped monitor and provide IV&V services to the U.S. Army's large new antiballistic missile (ABM) development program. Monitoring AT&T's performance on software development projects for the Army's missile defense system radars (Perimeter Acquisition Radar; PAR) was SAIC's most challenging software program by far at the time. This largely involved trade-off optimization studies on missile performance. These complex systems included the tracking radars used to follow the attacking missile in its terminal phase.

At the time, the U.S. Air Force and Army were competing against one another to be selected by the DOD to manage the new ABM defense program. The Huntsville missile developers had a different approach than the Air Force, but we were able to contribute to both efforts.

An area where we had problems in our ongoing efforts to capture large systems integration contracts was at Hanscom Air Force Base (headquarters of the Air Force Electronic Systems Division) near Boston. There were people at Hanscom that didn't particularly like SAIC, although we never knew why. These same people did however like Jim Palmer from Horizons Technology—a former SAIC physicist whom I came to know very well. Competing with Jim was not a good thing to do because of his stature at Hanscom, but I made some visits to Hanscom to convince the Air Force that they should give SAIC some business. Our solution as usual was to hire locally, starting with Marshall Cross, a very smart communications and intelligence guy. After a few years, Marshall decided to leave SAIC, but he left a legacy of competent people, including MIT engineer Don Tellage who played a key role in running Network Solutions at a time of crisis. He was a good manager who actually had successes at Hanscom, but nothing compared to Horizons Technology. These were painful days for me—I didn't like losing.

PUSHING ACROSS THE BORDERS

To maintain our high rate of growth, we increasingly looked overseas for business opportunities. For the most part, SAIC was asked to do work that was similar in content to what we were doing for the U.S. government. The main difference was that the generally acceptable bid rates in those days were higher for international work, and there was more contractual flexibility in dealing with us. Commercial and international codes of conduct varied quite a bit from country to country, however, and they concerned me.

The question for me was, why bother with international work at all? It was a way of broadening the company's scope—of enlarging our portfolio of business—and it also had a certain excitement to it. People like to go overseas and travel. And I felt we might be able to do very well financially. Telcordia had a fair amount of international business when it was acquired. I was hoping that we could coordinate our businesses so that when Telcordia was selling its telecommunication products they would also keep their eyes open for systems integration work for SAIC. Unfortunately, many of the staff at Telcordia resented SAIC doing anything in telecommunications systems integration. As it turned out, however, Hadi Bozorgmanesh was largely responsible for finding that work and he understood how to set up relationships between Telcordia and SAIC or with other companies, including Rolls Royce.

SAIC's earliest international work was performing training programs for the Kuwaiti defense forces, won by Charlie Stringfellow in 1976. We did some nuclear work with the Defense Aviation Repair Agency (DARA) organization in the United Kingdom. It was once part of Aldermaston, the United Kingdom's weapons development lab. It now is a separate company in which the U.K. government owns equity, along with its employees.* Harwell, a nuclear reactor technology-oriented organization, was the other major U.K. lab with which SAIC worked, introducing SAIC to another segment of the U.K. science community. Both laboratories were good partners for SAIC to team with in Europe, each providing unique technology missing from SAIC's portfolio.

I constantly worried about international work because of the sometimes questionable business ethics practiced in many countries. We kept trying to do business in Latin America but we had to be very careful to

---

*An ex-executive vice president of SAIC—Duane Andrews—is the CEO of its North American branch.

operate within all the complex international rules and regulations and the Foreign Corrupt Practices Act. As it turned out, we never were very successful.

But then there was Venezuela, and that was an entirely different story. In Venezuela, we had considerable success with work outsourced to us by Petroleos de Venezuela (PDVSA), the national oil company, even though some in the company were reluctant to outsource. However, the government changed, President Hugo Chavez came to power, we were wrongfully accused of being a tool of the Central Intelligence Agency, and our part of the new joint venture was expropriated. We barely got out of Venezuela before mob violence overtook the country. The manager of our joint venture was Roger Brown, located in Caracas, who together with others made sure we carried insurance for just that eventuality. We ended up recovering the book value for our holdings.

As part of the Bellcore (Telcordia) acquisition, SAIC inherited a business relationship with Telkom South Africa (TSA). Telcordia had been the software supplier for much of that phone company's operational software for their networks and had a strong relationship with Southwestern Bell in San Antonio. Southwestern Bell had a partial ownership in TSA. Bellcore (Telcordia) was selling a version of the software used by Southwestern Bell. We ended up using that software at TSA and then spent a considerable amount of time servicing it. TSA stopped payment on our work and lawsuits ensued both ways. They claimed they weren't getting the product they wanted, and we claimed that TSA wasn't paying their bills. We finally took it to the international court of appeals in The Hague, which ruled in our favor. But the South Africans never agreed to that decision and, when I left SAIC in 2004, it remained pending. The matter, however, was recently resolved in SAIC's favor by the South African courts.

The U.S. government occasionally wanted us to do international work, which led to another growth in business. In the company, the international opportunities that started expanding in the early 1990s were seen as an effective way to offset decreasing defense budgets. International work was performed by the group best suited to perform it. Mike Daniels oversaw the Middle East. Roger Brown and the energy folks had South America (including Venezuela) and part of Europe. Our commercial business in Europe was in the information technology and telecommunications markets. There was no one person responsible for all of SAIC's commercial work, and it was distributed widely throughout the company. This enhanced two-way technology transfer between government and commercial customers.

The Saudi contract became large with completion of the three major installations for the Royal Saudi Naval Forces (RSNF) in 1982. We then went into a maintenance and upgrade mode on which SAIC continues to perform. This is an excellent example of a very happy SAIC long-term customer. And we still have a happy customer today. Considering all our international work, I am most proud of the Saudi contract. It became a model of how to build a successful international relationship.

Other companies seemed to think that in dealing with the Saudis, the price should automatically be doubled because of all their oil money. SAIC did not do that. We charged the same as we charged everybody else. The Saudis knew that and appreciated our approach. Our business relationship with British Petroleum (BP) was also very favorable. Their projects were complex and always changing, so we needed to use only our best people. When they said change a program manager, we changed the program manager.

In Europe, we had SAIC-U.K., with its own president and business structure, which reported to the SAIC board or president. We hired as many people as we could through these foreign offices since it was usually less expensive. We quickly learned that it's not very cost-effective to jet five people back and forth across the Atlantic to do work when you can use talented locals to take care of it.

TURNING POINT: THE AMERICA'S CUP AND CORPORATE VISIBILITY

During the first couple of decades of SAIC's existence, we did little to promote the company to the news media or to anyone outside of our government contracting circle. Part of the reason was my own personal preferences—I am not one to toot my own horn. I much preferred to work quietly to satisfy our customers. Part of it was because of the fact that much of our work was highly classified, and we really couldn't talk much about it anyway. This all changed one fateful day in 1983.

For 132 years straight, America had never lost an America's Cup sailing competition. This was the longest winning streak in modern sports history until September 26, 1983—the day Dennis Conner's team lost the Cup to the challenger team from Australia. For close followers of the America's Cup races, this was a crushing defeat—not only because the Cup itself was lost to a foreign competitor, but also because it indicated that American hydrody-namics technology might no longer be first in the world.

I believed in the importance of the America's Cup, and I was confident that America could win back its namesake trophy. I knew such a feat was difficult but not impossible because of the work SAIC had done for the U.S. Navy on specialized hull designs. In his book *Comeback*, Dennis Conner de-scribes how Barry Shillito—a former assistant secretary of defense, member of the San Diego Yacht Club, and member of SAIC's board of directors—called Malin Burnham, who chaired the Sail America Foundation, to encour-age him to convince Dennis to meet with a team of naval architects and me at SAIC's La Jolla offices. According to Conner, he planned to limit the meet-ing to 30 minutes and get on with his business.

Dennis said it felt like he had to get by armed guards, watchdogs, and lead-lined walls to enter SAIC's offices. Dennis learned that SAIC was em-barrassed that the United States lost the America's Cup on technological grounds in 1983, and we explained that SAIC had the plans, technology, and ingenuity necessary to regain U.S. superiority. Dennis immediately de-cided to hire SAIC for his next attempt at the Cup. Says Dennis Conner, "The half-hour I had insisted on had turned into almost three hours, but it may have been the most productive time we spent in the early stages of the campaign."[2]

In the meeting with Dennis, we proposed to use revolutionary new computer-design methods never before attempted for complicated hull and keel design. Later Dennis noted, "SAIC pioneered a computer code that accu-rately predicted the wave-drag. I think this was a first in naval architec-ture."[3] He goes on to say how SAIC—working with a world-class team—also helped develop an accurate set of computer codes for the keel design. This was critical because it would show the best configuration from among many different options before boat construction. Ultimately, a design team was assembled, computer codes were successfully developed or modified, and the boats were built.

But the story didn't quite end there. In the preliminary races, the *Stars and Stripes* team was good but not dominating. Mother Nature can be fickle. A debate ensued over what should be done. Dennis had his opinion, and the naval architects had their own opinion based on a computer analysis that pointed to the need for a significant modification of the boat's winged keel. Ultimately, the architects prevailed. The keel was modified, and *Stars and Stripes*—with Dennis's extraordinary expertise—sailed to victory and took back the Cup.

Our deep involvement in the America's Cup put us in the public eye in a way that we had never before experienced. While this at first made me uncomfortable, I soon realized that the publicity was a very powerful and positive force for SAIC. It showed others that we were doing good things in our community and that SAIC was a progressive technology company that was on the leading edge of innovation. We earned a lot of good press, and we attracted an even greater number of talented scientists and engineers who wanted to work for a company like ours. The America's Cup brought us out of our shell, and we were a different, better company as a result.

10

The Loop:
Feedback and
Lessons Learned

*Most organizations have solved the problem of risk from individuals by
severely curtailing freedoms. That is not SAIC's intention. Rather, we will
continue to strive for a free and open company environment for the
majority of our employees by limiting freedom of decision for those with
poor judgment and by removing incurable cases.*

—from *Principles and Practices of SAIC*

As a loose federation of semiautonomous businesses, communication
was especially important in SAIC—not just to inform people about
what was happening up and down the organization, but also to act as an
essential ingredient in the glue that held it together. Communication
within the company was widespread, facilitated by SAIC's numerous committees and both formal and informal forums for exchanging information
and feedback, such as Meetings Week and the Management Council (discussed in detail in Chapter 6).

FEEDBACK: THE BREAKFAST
OF CHAMPIONS

At SAIC, there was a philosophy and a need for open communication throughout the organization. I strongly felt that the employees should and must be kept informed because they were the owners of the enterprise; any issue that affected the enterprise concerned them, although they might not be a direct part of the resolution. Managers often discussed such issues in staff meetings where employees might be able to suggest a new approach or solution.

Openness worked in both directions. Company leaders often received unrequested inputs from lower levels of the organization that helped them do their jobs. Regardless, to ensure that feedback flowed freely up, down, and across the organization (via line management and committees), there could be no punitive reaction to such input. Feedback was generally welcomed for the good ideas that were often generated. We were a networking company before most people knew what networking was.

For managers who were responsible for delivering results, feedback on performance was something they wanted early—and often. SAIC was unique in providing managers with a set of key metrics that were very simple to derive, that were very easy to understand, and that could be directly affected by things the managers and their employees did—or did not do—when working on contracts or in administrative roles. According to Cheryl Louie:

> Dr. Beyster had a fantastically simple management model, based on a couple of financial metrics that you had to deliver on. If you made your numbers, then you could do what you wanted. These key metrics were timesold—that is, the fraction of hours employees charged to billable contracts, versus company overhead—and PBT, profit before tax. And that was the beauty of the model—I could run my organization, make my targets, and then try experiments on the side. And if I was smart, I wouldn't try so many experiments that I missed my financial targets. Some people did miss their targets, and that was a problem for them.

While this simple feedback model served the company well for its first decade or two, business did get more complicated, and other metrics—particularly the F-factor formula, described in detail in Chapter 12—became important as well.

Beyond the financial and business feedback detailed previously, there were numerous other forums for communicating, sharing information, and giving and receiving feedback from others. We used every device we could think of to motivate employees to express themselves in a variety of forums at SAIC, hoping to pick up good ideas and to detect flaws in ongoing programs or in proposal efforts. Meetings Week was the most important forum we established for exchanging ideas. We scheduled preboard dinners so the employees and key managers had a place where they could meet the board members and express their feelings regarding actions the board was taking. Reflects Donna Cunningham:

> For those of us down in the trenches, Meetings Week was very useful. We learned what was going on in other sectors of the company, got a sense of overall direction, and met people we didn't ordinarily come in contact with. The stockholder's meeting was also useful.[1]

The value of Meetings Week as a networking and communications vehicle cannot be overstated. To say that forums such as these were an effective way to communicate and share feedback within the organization would be an understatement. Says Neil Hutchinson:

> When I first came to SAIC, I reacted to the Meetings Week process as an expensive perk that mostly was just a big social whirl. I discovered that nothing could be further from the truth. It was an important ingredient in the glue that kept this very decentralized organization from self-destructing. Management Council also made us all stop and look at where we'd been—and where we were going. It provided us with an opportunity to recognize the accomplishments of individuals from all levels of the company. Of course, it also provided an opportunity to chastise—there was nothing worse than having the biggest competitive loss for the quarter.

Meetings Week served a number of important purposes in SAIC, facilitating and improving unvarnished communications up, down, and across the organization; building teamwork and bonds between attendees; and bringing customers, potential key recruits, and other business partners into the company's inner circle. For a company that had roughly 1,000 divisions running somewhat autonomously, Meetings Week provided both the forum and the glue that helped to hold the company together.

LEARNING LESSONS FROM SUCCESSES AND FAILURES

The merging of SAIC's core scientific and engineering culture with its strong entrepreneurial spirit created an environment that didn't just encourage, but demanded, an in-depth analysis of the company's marketing and project successes and failures, just as scientists and engineers would deconstruct the result of any tests and experiments. The results of this analysis were incorporated into the company's proposal and project management systems to ensure that the lessons learned would have an immediate impact on the way SAIC pursued and conducted its business.

According to Matt Tobriner, the impetus for ferreting out lessons from SAIC's proposal and project initiatives came directly from the top:

> Of course, Bob was very interested in experiments, and learning from experiments. That's just his makeup from being a nuclear physicist. So he wanted us to pay a lot of attention to lessons learned, particularly in the area of marketing. Each quarter, at our Management Council meetings—and at other, smaller groupings—there was always an attempt to understand why we didn't do so well on something, whether it was a proposal or managing a project. Why did we lose that bid? How did this project get in trouble technically? What processes should we institute to avoid the same mistakes twice? There was a lot of emphasis on this process at the upper management level, and it crept down into the day-to-day activities of the company.

Lloyd Mosemann joined the company in February 1997, and our formal Lessons Learned program—in which he played the key role—was started shortly thereafter. In analyzing a series of procurement wins and losses in 1997, he observed a variety of nonpricing but recurring factors within SAIC's bids that contributed to a win or a loss. These factors were communicated to the rest of the company in the form of lessons learned. Says Mosemann:

> The most significant factors in our wins were relationships with the customer and past performance. However, we most often lost bids because we did not really know the customer, because there was a strong incumbent, because our proposals did not describe how we would accomplish the work, because of flawed teaming, because of personnel deficiencies,

and because of flaws in the proposal process. When I first started with SAIC, our Incumbency Win Rate was dismal. In recent years, we have typically won virtually all recompetes, whether measured as opportunities or dollars. I am certain our Lessons Learned program played a role in this improvement.

At Meetings Week, each manager could be assured that his or her performance—good or bad—would be highlighted for all to see. SAIC used the arrow technique. Each manager's name was put up on a board at the front of the group. Next to each manager's name was an arrow, pointing either up or down. Managers wanted their arrows to be pointing up, not down. Says John Glancy:

> The group didn't know if you were making 3 percent or −10 percent profit before tax, but if your arrow was down, you didn't want it down. You wanted it to be up, and there was a lot of peer pressure to have an up arrow. Lessons learned became a very important part of the company culture, so Bob made a point every time we got together in these meetings to pick on someone—usually for a mistake, but sometimes a winner. It might be something like, "Okay, Glancy, stand up and explain why we lost the bid to build a neutron radiography system." You then had to stand up and explain what happened. "Well, we didn't see the customer enough, we didn't write a good proposal, our price was too high." We would go through the whole thing and everybody would learn from our mistakes. This approach was used throughout the company so that everyone eventually knew what everyone else was doing.

As a result of this attention to learning lessons, SAIC started quality assurance programs and efforts to identify and dig deeply into problem contracts and projects, and to get managers out of their offices talking directly with customers. Most technical managers have an innate curiosity about what makes things tick, which makes them well suited to pointing out lessons learned from good and problem projects. But they sometimes have a tendency to prefer focusing on their technical tasks. I recognized this tendency and put pressure on managers to turn themselves outward—to SAIC's customers, to their coworkers, and to our executive team—rather than only inward to company projects. It was not acceptable for employees to act in isolation when their actions impacted others.

For my own part, I modeled this behavior whenever I could, spending much time calling and visiting customers—finding out what was going right and what might be going wrong with their contracts, and opening up channels of communication. I required my direct reports to provide me with a weekly activity report. I read every report every week, and asked questions about what I read. This stimulated managers to be prepared with answers.

Part of empowering employees and treating them like the owners they were was the need for them to accept responsibility for their actions and for the resulting outcomes, whether the outcomes were good, bad, or indifferent. In my mind, there was no room for excuses. Mistakes or failures were a natural part of our business, and to a degree they could be tolerated—especially when valuable lessons were learned. However, what I could not tolerate was an inability to accept responsibility for making a mistake. There were serious consequences for nonperformance, yet help, support, and "second chances" were available to employees who had performance problems, took responsibility for them, and sought help. SAIC employees must be accountable, for better or for worse.

It was a common practice for me to ask the individual opinion of many employees on a multitude of business topics, from the important to the mundane. In many of these cases, the questions were directed to employees who had little or no responsibility for the affected division. When I needed to speak to an employee, I ignored the hierarchy when I had to. I didn't feel that it made sense to go to someone's boss when it was much more efficient to go directly to the employee I wanted to communicate with. The telephone was therefore one of my greatest tools. If something in the organization bothered me, or if I thought I could help in some way, I wouldn't hesitate to pick up the phone and call any employee, anywhere, at any time to try to keep things moving. In this way, I tried to keep my finger firmly on the pulse of the organization, and I knew what people were doing and how projects were going. I knew who I could trust, and I knew who would know the most about a particular topic. In addition, having a "chat with the old man" was usually a feather in an employee-owner's cap, even if the content was less than great.

TURNING POINT: FIXED-PRICE WORK

All the best people with lots of freedom to build won't make a company successful if it underbids on fixed-price work. This was demonstrated with one particular SAIC program—the Large Area Tracking Range (LATR). On a fixed-price contract like LATR—which requires the contractor to deliver a specific product or service at a set price—correction of deficiencies may be expensive and can lead to a sizable financial loss.

LATR's original scope was to develop a Navy range tracking system to measure the performance of naval aircraft in simulated battle conditions at four range sites—two in the Atlantic Ocean, and two in the Pacific Ocean. The contract also included delivery of a Portable Tracking System, an Air Combat Maneuvering System, documentation support, and the production of 341 Participant Instrumentation Packages. These tasks entailed the development and integration of both hardware and software—a difficult undertaking. The risk was compounded by the fact that the Navy wanted a fixed-price contract for this work.

Administered by Dick Wallner, A-20 was SAIC's standardized review approach to evaluating and managing the cost and risk contained in a fixed-price bid. In this particular case, the bidding organization had some experience in bidding and executing a program with similar but lesser scope—the Range Operational Control System, also for the Navy. SAIC's bid was $53 million for the proposed fixed-price contract—a figure that in retrospect appeared to be inadequate. SAIC's main competitor—Cubic—had bid $73 million for the same contract, $20 million more than SAIC's bid.

As a result of a more detailed understanding of the program—and recognizing the company's reputation was at stake—corporate recommitted to the customer that SAIC would satisfy the basic contract requirements. The customer agreed to a revised schedule and SAIC estimated that it would overrun the contract by $22 million.

The program was restaffed as the most important initial remedial step, assigning a new, Navy-experienced program manager, a strong chief systems engineer (CSE), adding additional qualified systems engineering staff, and establishing a proper systems engineering process. SAIC rescheduled and recosted the entire effort. Subcontractor renegotiations were necessary and difficult. We spoke with key subcontractors, exhorting them to rejoin the bid team. One subcontract, difficult to manage under a fixed-price arrangement, was renegotiated to a time-and-materials contract (a contract that sets fixed, hourly prices for labor, and provides for reimbursement of other expenses by the government at their cost). This approach ultimately proved successful.

As a result of the proactive teaming among the program team, subcontractors, the customer, and SAIC, the program concluded successfully with technical requirements being met, the revised schedule being accomplished, and contract terms satisfied. The customer ultimately rated the program as purple, the highest possible rating.

This episode—and others like it—caused us to reevaluate and strengthen our bidding and management processes for fixed-price work and had a major impact on the way we thought about the company and the freedom provided to our line managers. We learned there had to be a very stringent top-level, cross-cutting discipline involved. And it pointed out big gaps in our systems engineering expertise and processes for designing complex software/hardware systems at the time. We also learned that when all's not well on a contract, it can be made well with the right management intervention, but be prepared to spend company money.

11

The Wild Card: Experiment Constantly

Internal competition has always been a complex matter at SAIC, as it is in most companies in which aggressive, entrepreneurial people abound. Success through unfair competition and unfair tactics should not be rewarded at SAIC. That does not mean that it has never happened, but it is not our policy. Success through cooperation, through combining the best talents of our people will be encouraged and rewarded.

—from Principles and Practices of SAIC

When Thomas Edison was trying to invent a new way to store energy for long periods of time, it took him more than 50,000 tries (and more than $1 million of his own money) before he got it right, resulting in the world's first successful nickel-iron-alkaline storage battery. Edison's basic design is still used today, and his persistence at experimenting until making a breakthrough remains a quintessential example for all scientists and engineers who seek new approaches and solutions to complex problems. With degrees of persistence, an open mind, and a dose of intuitively inspired luck—remarkable things can be and are achieved through the process of experimentation.

Such was the culture at SAIC, which was for much of its existence fundamentally a science and technology company, run and staffed by scientists, engineers, and other technologists. But instead of experimenting with light bulbs and batteries, SAIC's employees experimented with their organization—adding a new location here, reorganizing a division there—and with its programs, projects, and methods. While other companies worried about maintaining stability across their existing lines of business, SAIC's technical managers were figuring out how they could try new ideas. Through this trail-and-error approach, small projects often became large, multiyear programs—contributing to the company's dramatic and sustained growth.

Experimentation and informed risk taking were trademarks of the SAIC style. These features of SAIC's business philosophy were core ingredients in the company's growth.

SAIC: IDEA LABORATORY

In SAIC's culture of ideas, the best idea—the one that provided the most effective solution, considering cost and technical excellence—usually won. I made a point of encouraging ideas to come from anywhere in the organization—when it came to an idea, there were no walls. Divisions occasionally competed against one another to win a contract from the same customer, sometimes confusing the customer and aggravating the division managers who had submitted competing proposals. SAIC's business culture was very Darwinian, with the best ideas (and teams) surviving—and thriving—and the weaker ideas being pushed aside.

Part and parcel of the freedom to pursue your business interests was the reality that everyone had to accept some personal responsibility for their own job and their own future. Freedom came without guarantees—employees had to keep producing and continue to prove themselves. This made SAIC a highly competitive environment in which to work. Potential competitions between divisions and groups became apparent at SAIC's annual planning meetings, which required such conflicts to be sorted out before they became destructive to the organization or customers. Says Richard Shearer (a leader in our Navy business and head of the Ethics Committee):

> When I attended the annual planning sessions at which Dr. Beyster had the group heads lay out their plans for the year ahead, I would often notice— as would Bob—that the plans overlapped. My interests were in Navy con- tracts. That meant separating Dick Eger's group plans from Carl Albero's, and ensuring that they did not "shop" each others' customers. When an overlap was noticed, it would be brought to Bob's attention and usually re- solved by him. I once told Bob that SAIC was like the Serengeti Plain— when the game was plentiful, we hunted in cooperative packs, but when the game was slim, we hunted each other.

One way I controlled the negative effects of internal competition was through my direct and personal control of a pool of discretionary funds. Managers who needed some of these funds to kick off a new initiative—or to remain profitable and achieve financial targets for the year—knew that the quid pro quo was to not become a source of or- ganizational conflict. Similarly, top executives and I would personally resolve major bid or no-bid decisions and decide who would take the lead when competing groups could not resolve the issues themselves. Working through these contentious issues often involved multiple meet- ings, where I would ask members of the two sides penetrating questions about their decision logic before deciding one way or the other. While potentially destructive, this internal competition ensured that SAIC could quickly adapt to changing market forces more rapidly than other large competitors.

Our philosophy was that the organizational structure should not interfere with doing the best job on our projects. It should encourage and reward use of the best people and their capabilities. Creating the right alignment of people and organizational structures to best serve the customer required me to assess where the best ideas were coming from, and then to regularly reorganize the company so that the right people were in the right places to meet our business needs and objectives, and to maintain clarity of focus on our customers' needs—making the organi- zation stronger and more effective in the process. And I did this at least once a year.

"This is one of those days when I have half a mind to implode the corporate structure."

This is quite a different mode of operation from many of our competitors, which often put all of their commercial business in one dedicated subsidiary or entity. While we may have focused our large, riskier fixed-price contracts in specific groups or sectors set up to handle them, we did not arbitrarily move work around the organization. The reason to do so had to be a good one, such as our commercial work was similar enough to our government work that we were able to use the same people and skills. According to Tom Darcy, SAIC executive vice president of strategic projects and former CFO:

Bob unfailingly did annual reorganizations of business units in the late fall of each year, and he did so to make sure they were positioned to start each new fiscal year with the right functional skills to best address their respective customer needs. The overarching design goal was to make sure the company always had the right resources in the right places to deploy against the government's biggest challenges. It was very common for people to be redeployed from serving customers in one agency market to customers in an altogether different agency market if their same technical skills were in higher demand there. During this annual reorganization process, Bob also had a way of taking the weaker performing business units, dividing them up, and moving the pieces into stronger business units to help them learn to be successful. Whatever the driver, this reorganization exercise was a very key factor in the company's financial success. It invariably created consternation for the affected organization, and that kind of annual tension became a highly anticipated part of the culture. It was something that everybody knew would happen every year, and people embraced it because they knew in the end it would make us stronger.

Reorganizations occurred for various reasons: to pursue new markets, to create teams to solve particularly complex technical problems, or to give someone a chance to move up the leadership chain. And when changes didn't have the desired effect on organizational performance, I started the experiment over again. We learned from failure and tried another approach.

SAIC's highly competitive, Darwinian business environment had inevitable backlashes. There were times when divisions refused to cooperate with one another, unless ordered to do so by me or other top executives. In a way, this was as it was supposed to be. Managers were expected to focus on—and were rewarded for—growing their own business, not the business of another manager. If there was a business reason for managers to cooperate, they would. However, as the company grew, it became increasingly necessary for divisions to band together to win larger competitions. This had the effect of turning some of the company's most uncooperative managers into models of teamwork.

In their book *Hot Groups: Seeding Them, Feeding Them, and Using Them to Ignite Your Organization*, authors and university professors Jean Lipman-Blumen and Harold J. Leavitt describe something that they call a "hot group." According to the authors, hot groups are not just a new name for a team or task force, but an entirely new state of mind, "an attitude that brings real people together around an invigorating challenge, inspiring them to meet that challenge through an extraordinary combustion of creativity, passion, exhilaration, determination, and ordinary perspiration."[1]

Lipman-Blumen and Leavitt worked with me in SAIC's early days, providing business consulting services and guidance. However, as the authors describe in their book, they learned a lesson or two from the company they were hired to help:

> We once worked with Science Applications International (SAIC), a California company that is now quite large. . . . Dr. Beyster built his organization by searching the nation, and later the world, for struggling but promising little hot groups of scientists. Leaving them wherever he found them, he invited them to join the company. "Joining" simply meant that he provided each group with enough of a financial umbrella to let it carry on with its beloved tasks until it bore both scientific and financial fruit.
>
> A few years after he began, we counted twenty-three such groups in SAIC, in as many different locations. As consultants, we gravely advised Dr. Beyster that he just couldn't go on in that helter-skelter way. He'd better get all these scattered bits and pieces organized and controlled. Fortunately—and characteristically—he ignored us. The company, a company not so much of individuals as of groups, now has upwards of 400 such units, far more widely scattered. Despite our initial doomsday forecasts, SAIC continues to prosper.[2]

Our form of employee ownership and participation made SAIC develop as it has, coupled with our dedication to hire the very best people and make a real effort to promote and retain them. It instilled that little something extra that drove many people (not all) to try harder, care more, worry about the company, think about the company's welfare, strategize, and even cooperate to accomplish specific company objectives. The more specific the objective, the more these ad hoc teams of really talented people drove themselves to win. Each win brought new capabilities and new challenges, many of which we were ill prepared to handle.

SAIC's business units became hothouses of ideas. The company did not establish artificial rules on the size of an acceptable contract—if an employee could bring in sufficient revenues to cover one person, or a whole team, SAIC provided the supporting cast of contracts and finance staff. SAIC was a constantly changing organization. If a division wasn't changing along with the organization, they could fall behind—which meant someone else had an opportunity to take their place.

Everyone seemed to be looking for a new way of doing things—a new customer, a new meeting, a new organization, a new committee, and so forth. One prime example was our yearly reorganization, orchestrated by Jim Idell and others. Groups were added, subtracted, combined, and moved, as were key people. The process was almost always customer and marketing driven. Another example was the creation of Company 6, SAIC's mid- to low-rate entity, which didn't exist until the early 1990s. Company 1 bid rates didn't work well against some key competitors, so SAIC lowered its rates for certain services and situations to become more competitive—leading to the establishment of Company 6.

SAIC's Companies within the Company

SAIC created a number of *companies* matrixed into sectors and groups. These companies provided a flexible approach to responding to different bidding rate opportunities. Divisions with similar resource and customer requirements were designated to be in the same company. Company 1 and 6 were the core SAIC companies for most government contracting and Company 21 was focused on commercial customers. Most sectors or groups with Company 1 divisions also had divisions operating in Company 6.

Company 1, SAIC Research and Development Company, was the full-rate company, which allowed for overhead to be invested in R&D, lower timesold, a competitive fringe benefit package, and fixed on- and off-site overhead structures. Divisions with large research, design, development, and systems integration contracts frequently fit best in this company.

Company 6, Technology Services Company, was the low-cost company, which best fit divisions facing increased competitive pressure in the technical services markets such as operations, maintenance, and outsourcing. Company 6 was ideal for businesses with large, multiple-year, cost-reimbursable contracts. The overhead was tailored to the requirements of a specific contract and the fringe packages were designed to meet the varying needs of employees. Lower costs were achieved as a result of a number of factors, including work being performed on the customer site, lower marketing costs due to long duration contracts, and fewer contract or administrative resources required due to the type of work being performed.

RISK, RECOVERY,
REORGANIZATION, REPUTATION

It's impossible to build and grow an organization like SAIC without taking risks. I expected managers to aggressively pursue success in their organizations, but to act for the good of the company. This approach led to making some mistakes along the way, and everyone in the organization made their share. But except for breaches in ethics and integrity, the company had an uncommon tolerance for trial and error that applied to every aspect of the organization. Trying new things, attacking a new market, changing the company's organizational structure, and pursuing other experiments often meant not getting it exactly right—especially the first time. But this was just one step in SAIC's approach to experimentation, and more often than not it led to ingenious solutions.

Recovery might involve incremental, iterative adjustments or a 180-degree turn. According to Mark Hughes (who joined SAIC in 1990, grew a small systems development and integration business to over $1 billion, and put together a course on SAIC's culture—which he taught within the company more than 100 times), the company's penchant for experimentation started at the top. Says Hughes:

> I always got the sense from Dr. Beyster that he considered every decision he made to be an experiment. I think this is one of the most important factors in the success of SAIC. In many companies, a decision made by senior management was viewed as a commandment from God, to be followed blindly. One of Dr. Beyster's favorite cartoons is the one where he is showing the way, but all the employees, down below, are each headed in their own directions. By viewing our decisions as experiments, it encouraged timely decision making, followed by monitoring and redirecting quickly when necessary. Other companies often go down the wrong path for a long time because they are following orders from on high. SAIC moved quickly and decisively at every level because we were willing to make mistakes and correct them.

Going hand in hand with SAIC's scientific culture and love for experimentation was a flexible organization with matrixed relationships between projects and divisions. Although assigned to a particular division, employ-

Pointing the Way
Courtesy of Bob and Betty Beyster. Reprinted with permission.

ees followed the contracts and went to where the work was. If one division
needed someone from a different division to help out on a contract for a period of time, deals were made to provide contract coverage for defined periods of time at a certain dollar ceiling. Commitments were taken as seriously
as signing a contract because delivering the level of effort often made the
difference in satisfying the contract deliverables. Those who developed a
reputation for reneging on commitments found that there was little pa-
tience. Conversely, those who became trusted colleagues never worried
about running out of coverage.

The company—particularly in the early days—was very unstructured at
times and, while it never devolved into full-blown chaos, the organization
could sometimes be described as chaotic. Those employees who depended
on a strict hierarchy to provide guidance and direction soon discovered that
SAIC's free-form and fast-changing organization provided few places to
hang onto, and they were not likely to stay with the company for very long.
For those who thrived on freedom and the excitement that comes with a

slightly unpredictable but often rewarding environment, it was just right and long-term careers were made and legacies forged.

Gradually, thriving businesses were built not only with relevant technical agencies but also with those supporting our large military establishment and its supporting structure. Later in our growth, the company ventured into specialized services with the intelligence community. This was extremely difficult to initiate since we usually needed particular security clearances to perform the work.

Small contracts gave us a foothold with new customers as our employees offered unique talents and developed a reputation for quality work. In many cases, if our work wasn't good enough, we would repeat it until it was. This required the development of an outstanding contracts and legal staff to make sure we always tried hard, within reason, to please the customers. Chuck Nichols was the first of such people.

SAIC ended up building a very good reputation doing a multitude of projects leveraging our previous experiences. These are unfortunately too numerous to do justice to. I therefore try to dwell on some of the main themes and as many of the key players as I can, but, in the process, many of them could unfortunately be overlooked.

In the first year of SAIC's history, we grew to 20+ people. This included people largely from General Atomic with weapons effects expertise such as Don Huffman, Jerry Pomraning, Charlie Stevens, and a group leaving Convair led by Dan Hamlin and Bob Lowen who worked on projects involving infrared emissions from nuclear weapons. They analyzed data from old nuclear weapons tests in Nevada and Enewetok Island in the South Pacific. Both groups in the first year brought in their friends who sold contract research business where SAIC was an incumbent contractor, as well as selling new work.

In our second year, several strategic hires occurred—Gene Ray stood out as being the most aggressive builder. He hired primarily from the Los Angeles area and from aerospace corporations like TRW and rapidly grew the mission analysis or trade-off area with the U.S. Air Force. The company developed and improved a very versatile set of mission trade-off tools so the Air Force could determine how to design new missiles as well as missile silo shielding against a Soviet ballistic missile attack. Our design tools were state of the art and gave us a leg up on our competitors.

As a fresh organization with fresh ideas, we were good at helping the Air Force sell their overall capabilities to the government in both Los Angeles and Washington. Eventually, these same capabilities were sold to both the Army and Air Force from our Huntsville and Washington offices. New employees wanted nice offices and also wanted exciting and rewarding career paths in the SAIC organization. These employees also wanted autonomy in developing their businesses. Since the new offices were key to meaningful growth with customers, we tried hard to accommodate these employees. The remote offices were susceptible to splintering and much of my time was spent in helping these outposts so we could preserve our embryonic marketing inroads in the regional businesses.

As the company grew, the process for lending employees to other divisions to perform needed work became less casual and more formal. With tens of thousands of employees working on thousands of different contracts, this became a necessity to ensure that commitments were tracked and employees charged their time against the correct contracts. This more formalized process included using memoranda of understanding to record the commitments that managers made, and to ensure all parties were clear about expected levels of effort to meet contract schedules and deliverables.

Ideas for new projects and programs came from throughout the organization. While sometimes I might suggest a new hire who had detailed relevant experience in a target agency—especially in an agency such as the Federal Aviation Administration or the Federal Bureau of Investigation, where SAIC was establishing new business—most often the ideas came from below.

There was a groundswell of ideas at SAIC because we were bringing so many bright people into the company. We were flooded with internal requests for development money. That's one thing that was great about SAIC. We were overwhelmed with ideas and never had to sit around and ask, "Is there some new business to pursue?" We always had new topics for proposals. It's like sailing. Many people spend a lot of time working on a plan, but they're so busy working on the plan, and charting their direction, that the boat never leaves the dock. Our boat usually got away from the dock promptly. Where we were going wasn't always clear. But if it looked like we were going to run into a sandbar or encounter a storm, we simply turned, and moved in a new direction.

TURNING POINT: LEVERAGING EXISTING TECHNOLOGY INTO SOLUTIONS WITH NATIONAL SIGNIFICANCE

I constantly emphasized during my tenure at the helm of SAIC keeping our customers' needs front and center in our minds and in our actions. I also challenged our managers and technologists to find ways to leverage exist-ing technology into entirely new solutions for our customers' persistent problems. One such outcome of our focus on customers and leveraging ex-isting technology into new solutions is SAIC's Integrated Container Inspec-tion System (ICIS).

The 4 million+ large shipping containers used to transport goods around the world—and into American ports—are vulnerable to terrorist at-tacks. These containers are for the most part unsecured and constantly at risk of unauthorized access, giving terrorists the opportunity to deliver a small nuclear device to any major port. Only a fraction of the containers en-tering the country are inspected—no more than about 6 percent—relying mostly on experience and hoping that any such weapons will be caught. The reasons for this lack of 100-percent inspection are many, including lack of sufficient funding for necessary Homeland Security programs, and grave concerns on the part of the shipping industry that transport of containers through the ports will be slowed to an unacceptable level.

SAIC's ICIS offers a way to meet this challenge—allowing 100-percent inspection of shipping containers with minimal slowdown of containers through ports in which they are deployed. Pulling together technology from many different areas in the company, including high-speed gamma ray im-aging using the company's Vehicle and Cargo Inspection System (VACIS), ra-diation scanning, and optical character recognition (OCR) capabilities, ICIS can scan high volumes of containers in the normal flow of traffic at the gates or on the quay. Just as important, ICIS can integrate data from these and many other sources, including the terminal's security, automation, and management systems, for use in security and productivity applications.

According to Vic Orphan, a fellow physicist and an SAIC Senior vice president for corporate development, the government's methodology shows room for improvement. Says Orphan:

U.S. Customs' standard operating mode was to initially inspect only 2 or 3 percent of the containers. Later, after security levels were raised, they were doing maybe 5 or 6 percent on average. If the containers were com-ing from a known shipper or a relatively safe port, they would do minimal inspection. If they were looking for drugs—which is what they were mainly looking for before 9/11—and if a shipment was from Colombia, then they would probably do a 20-percent inspection because of the high probability of drug smuggling. The problem with that approach if you are trying to prevent the importation of a nuclear weapon or nuclear materials is that it is a very rare event. And, unlike drugs—of which there could be thousands of smuggling attempts—there are not that many nuclear weapons around, and it is going to be a one-time event. The terrorists are not stupid—they are not going to send it from Karachi, Pakistan. They are going to send it from a safe port, and they are going to bribe someone to move it through. It will probably be in a shipment of tennis shoes.

What this analysis indicates is that the nation's strategy for container inspection is inadequate for the most lethal threats, and until this problem is fully addressed, our nation will be vulnerable to attack.

SAIC developed ICIS to use the latest detection technology against the container inspection problem. It was the classic SAIC experimental approach: understand the nature of the problem (no container security), experiment with potential solutions (detectors used in many ways), and develop a technology that is affordable and effective. ICIS integrates the terminal's existing systems and can be implemented with minimal impact on terminal operations. It could provide a vital first line of defense against terrorist threats.

Building ICIS involved extensive cross-collaboration within SAIC, pulling together technologies from across the company—image processing experts in Tucson, barcode tracking technologies from Kansas City, and database experts from San Diego. One of the most extraordinary aspects of ICIS, however, is that it became a product—an inspection system that can be sold on a per-unit basis for port security customers in the United States and around the world. This experiment in product design and development worked at SAIC, despite a lack of experience in the products marketplace, because ICIS built on SAIC's core strengths:

- Technical expertise
- Focus on critical problems facing the nation
- Customer-driven philosophy to satisfy customer needs
- Total commitment to system design and deployment that is affordable and minimally disruptive to existing operating environments

ICIS shows how decades of persistent experimentation with a strong user focus transformed innovative solutions into a higher-volume business with national significance. While it cannot stop every possible threat, it is one more tool that can be used to improve the security of our nation.

12

The Bottom Line: Expect Reasonable Profit with Stock Price Growth

Our objective is that profits after tax should be in the 3 percent to 4 percent range. This is reasonable and sufficient to make SAIC an attractive investment to its employees and to provide the resources necessary to build the company—prime reasons why SAIC is not a nonprofit organization. The profits made over and above that objective can be invested in the company's people and its future. There are two "profit pools," one involving bonus awards of stock or dollars to a wide range of people in the company (not focused on the few) and the other used to invest in projects to enhance the company's future.

—from Principles and Practices of SAIC

SAIC was a profit-making organization, but not to the exclusion of the other values—doing what was ethically right, contributing to the national good, creating a good place to work—that were important to the company and its employee-owners. SAIC needed profit to advance its stock price, reward employees, and generate discretionary funds to be used to seed new initiatives, but the company's profit goals were modest, and there was little reason for employees to get overly stressed—except when they missed them.

A FAIR PROFIT—NOTHING MORE, NOTHING LESS

My philosophy from the beginning—which became company policy—was that SAIC should make a fair profit from its business. The business was not a nonprofit—so losses weren't acceptable—but neither was the business out to make a quick buck at the expense of its mostly government customers. From the beginning, I saw SAIC as in a partnership with its customers—one that would build long-term, mutually beneficial relationships that would enable the company to provide great talent at a reasonable price. And because the company was employee owned—and privately held—the company didn't have outside shareholders demanding that profits be generated at the expense of these other core values of the company.

The standard notion of profit is that it is a reward for taking risk—the riskier a venture, then the greater the profit should be. Many of SAIC's contracts were—particularly in the early years—cost plus fixed fee; that is, the government would reimburse all of our out-of-pocket costs and then award us a fixed negotiated fee. These contracts were of relatively low risk to the company and our negotiated profits were also relatively low. In some cases, contracts were firm fixed price. We negotiated a bottom-line contract amount that we had to live with no matter how much our costs were. These were by nature of relatively high risk to the company, and our negotiated profits were significantly higher. When we developed new products, the upfront investment of our time and money—coupled with the very real risks of failure—generally required even higher profits.

Our philosophy of making a reasonable profit permeated the organization. Employees were able to deal with customers more comfortably because there was no pressure to generate high profits. With government clients, who themselves might never benefit from the rewards of private industry, SAIC employees never felt they were exploiting the people who employed them. As an added benefit, employees participated in exciting and meaningful programs and exercised a degree of independence and autonomy that was rare in other defense contractors. Although many employees were motivated by the stock ownership (which is why the "glue" worked), SAIC offered other benefits that went beyond the financial incentives. Says Sydell Gold:

> I believe that for most of the people I worked with, the psychic value one got from doing a good job was the most important thing. The money came as an ancillary benefit. The main reward is you may have discovered something new, or you may have applied something in a way people hadn't thought of before, and you had fun while you were doing it. And Bob Beyster let it be known that he thought what we were doing was important.

If a division was going to survive and thrive in SAIC's intensely competitive environment, it had to have more than a great idea and happy customers—it also had to achieve certain financial targets. These targets were predictable and reasonable, especially when compared to other (especially product) businesses where profit margins several times SAIC's expected targets were the norm.

The key metrics included revenue growth from year to year. The goal for profit before tax was static for 15 years at 6 percent for our government business. In the commercial space, 7 or 8 percent was typical, and eventually our government business profit target increased to 7 percent. Another key metric was proposal submittals—the total value of proposals submitted during the year. The target for proposal submittals was four times revenue. This pointed up the fact that if the divisions weren't writing many proposals, they weren't going to meet their revenue and profit goals. The proposal win rate was also important. We had a relatively low win rate in the early days for a government contractor because we were so diversified—if a division had a 40 percent to 50 percent win rate, we thought they were terrific. Eventually, the win rate became 70 percent. The fourth metric was accounts receivable—the money that had been billed to customers but not yet received. Accounts receivable had to be 60 days of revenue or less.

INTERNAL INVESTMENT STRATEGIES

The use of discretionary resources to invest in company growth was an important tool for driving performance throughout the SAIC organization. SAIC used a variety of budgeting methods to manage its profit and loss (P&L) centers, which might hold 10 to 300 employees each:

- *Budget elasticity:* Budgets were scaled to the volume of the business base. For example, if during a reporting year a division or group grew beyond their annual revenue plan, they were allocated the majority of the extra overhead (OH) and general and administrative (G&A) funds to continue growing the business. If the division chose not to spend it, their internal profit would be increased by the amount of underspending and their bonus pool computation would be enhanced. Similarly, if the division underachieved the growth in their annual plan, their scaled OH and G&A budgets declined, possibly forcing a reduction in spending to meet their profit target.

- *P&L taxation:* The internal management (P&L) reporting, while providing OH and G&A budgets scaled to increasing or decreasing business volumes, allocated a small portion of that budget from each division, nicking its profit slightly. The allocated budget was accumulated at the corporate level to dole out to meaningful initiatives that a specific division might not have been able to afford on its own without underachieving its profit plan. This accomplished two objectives: (1) It allowed corporate initiatives to be funded in addition to some of the important grassroots division initiatives; and (2) it gave me access to both resources and investment ideas. These were important to technology and business development.

THE F-FACTOR: DRIVING BOTTOM-LINE PERFORMANCE

As a scientist, I knew from personal experience that numbers—hard, measurable, quantitative standards—drive employee performance. As owners, the company's employees had a very personal stake in their company's performance. The better they performed, the better the company performed— helping to achieve a higher stock price and broaden the available opportunities.

But how did employees know that what they did today would result in a stock price increase months into the future? Peter Pavlics, SAIC's comptroller, led the effort to develop a tool for allocating bonuses that linked employee performance with metrics supporting stock price growth that we called the F-factor formula. The F-factor formula was comprised of the key metrics that drove the company. This new set of metrics included revenue growth and profit rate, including a cost of capital charge to motivate good balance sheet management (e.g., good receivables management). These pairings were plotted on a chart so that anyone could readily see exactly what combination of revenue growth and profit percentage—say, 16 percent revenue growth and a 7 percent profit margin on that growth—would help drive a 10 percent to 12 percent overall growth in the company's stock price.

Hitting the target earned the division an F-factor of 1.0. But, if they could do even better—say, revenues came in higher than the 16 percent target used in the previous example—then the group could earn an F-factor of 1.2 or 1.3 or more—up to 2.0—resulting in more bonus for the group. Some businesses were in markets that couldn't generate that kind of revenue growth. They could, however, generate a higher profit margin. The F-factor formula accounted for the trade-off in revenue growth versus profit rate—divisions could achieve a 1.0 F-factor with relatively low revenue growth so long as their profit rate was sufficient to push up the F-factor. Conversely, a division with relatively low profit rate could make up for it with higher revenue growth. There was a direct trade-off. So it was totally acceptable for a group to generate less revenue as long as they brought their target profit to the bottom line.

According to Tom Darcy, the message was clear: meet or exceed your F-factor targets, and you will be rewarded. Says Darcy:

> The bonus pools were built around the F-factor concept and related targets for year-over-year revenue and profit growth. The targets were designed to achieve the performance necessary to support a double-digit percentage of annual stock price growth. Everything else fell from that. Bonuses were earned at all levels of the organization and were allocated to employees from the pools by managers at each of these levels. On an overall basis, bonuses were designed to be paid 50 percent in cash, 25 percent in vested stock for the short-term portion, and 25 percent in four-year vesting stock for the long-term portion. High performance by employees was also rewarded with four-year vesting stock options as an additional long-term incentive, which further enabled them to participate in the continued growth of the company.

Managers were highly motivated to generate an F-factor in excess of 1.0 through their own performance—generating the combination of revenue growth and profit rate that would result in stock price growth in the desired range of from 10 percent to 15 percent while increasing their own bonus pools. As it turns out, this stock price growth was very good compared to other conservative financial investments. Indeed, it was just strong enough and secure enough—and the F-factor formula simple enough—that most managers were motivated to make it happen. Because all managers were owners, they closely followed the company's stock and value growth and did whatever they could to help achieve or even exceed the year's target.

To determine the specific target stock price increase for a given year, I assessed market conditions with my senior management team. The general rule of thumb was to achieve 10 percent to 15 percent stock price growth. There were years when our booming commercial business doubled our expected profit targets.

I also factored in the budgets submitted by SAIC's business units. All business units went through the annual planning process that required an analysis of how they thought their businesses would do for the year—particularly in the way of planned revenues. If they wanted to undertake major marketing initiatives that their own resources wouldn't cover, they endeavored to get on my guideline list.

For managers working hard to make their F-factor targets, there were a number of simple but powerful variables they could employ to help generate the kind of profits that they needed. Perhaps the most important metric was *timesold,* which, as we have previously discussed, is the ratio of direct labor dollars incurred working on contracts to the total labor dollars incurred in a specific period of time.

Working with SAIC's financial analysis specialists, I knew that in order for a business unit to achieve its plans, it would have to run at a timesold of 75 percent. This means that, on average, the business unit's employees were charging 75 percent of their collective time on the job to customer contracts, and 25 percent to overhead activities. We would then use exception reports to track the performance of each business unit on timesold, and other key metrics. If all of a sudden an exception report (published every two weeks) showed that a particular business unit was running at 72 percent instead of the planned 75 percent, it immediately became obvious that there was a problem, and action had to be taken to first understand why this variance from plan had occurred, and then correct it.

There were legitimate reasons why a business unit might have a lower timesold percentage than anticipated. The unit might be bidding larger programs, or its contract mix might have changed. But if the staff wasn't being used productively, then this was an indication that certain business managers had problems that needed to be fixed and that action should be taken. Tracking timesold was a very effective way to quickly get at problems in the cost control of labor, since labor was the greatest cost for SAIC.

SAIC has traditionally operated on 13, four-week accounting periods throughout the year. At each period end, there would be a complete operating report of all the key metrics. SAIC's financial staff visited or contacted each of the operating units and went through the key metrics in the report, identifying what had happened during the accounting period. In addition, SAIC's CFO made a regular presentation to brief me on the company's financial status, highlighting potential problems and opportunities. Says Tom Darcy:

> Each month we would sit down with Bob and go through a complete financial review of the company. In addition to more traditional reviews of revenues, contract performance, and areas of business opportunities and risks, we would also review where business units might be missing key operating metric goals such as those for timesold or accounts receivable. There was a process for business units to identify and act on the problem metrics they were worrying about and, if they didn't, there was also a process to try to identify these types of problems early on at the corporate level. Help from Bob could come in different forms depending on the situation, but in all cases people know he would be quick to act on early warnings.

When businesses were struggling, the first priority was to understand the problem and to assign people to try to help the struggling business unit. If the problem ultimately couldn't be solved or the issue turned around, my view was "We gave it our best shot—chalk it up to experience." I could be very patient with people who asked for help, and I would bring all the resources of the company to bear on a problem. But I was quite impatient with people who were not transparent or not willing to reach out for help.

TURNING POINT: POST-COLD WAR NATIONAL SECURITY PROGRAMS

The collapse of the Soviet Union in 1991 meant that the Cold War was officially over. While defense contractors and the American public enthusiastically celebrated this seemingly impossible event, for the many companies that had built their long-term business plans on the assumption of a Cold War without end, everything suddenly changed. Once the reality of the situation hit policymakers, it didn't take long for them to realize that U.S. defense budgets could be dramatically scaled back, resulting in a "peace dividend" that could be redirected to social programs or to spur economic growth. For contractors like SAIC that relied heavily on Department of Defense (DOD) programs for their growth and profitability, this meant that something else would have to replace the defense business that would soon be lost.

Perhaps at least in part because of its unique organizational structure based on autonomous, fast, and flexible business units, SAIC's bottom line did not suffer for long. After the end of the Cold War, the company's government business continued to increase. What changed, however, was the nature of the work that SAIC performed.

Before the end of the Cold War, much of SAIC's policy analysis work was in the area of arms control, and understanding the motives and intentions of the superpowers. As the threat of global confrontation with the Soviets faded away in the post-Cold War era, regional conflicts came to the fore, along with threat reduction and nonproliferation of nuclear capability, and keeping nuclear, chemical, and biological weapons out of the hands of unstable or unfriendly regimes. Reflecting this shift, SAIC's Center for Verification Research—created in 1989 under a contract sponsored by the Defense Nuclear Agency—moved in that direction.

An issue of particular concern in the wake of the dissolution of the Soviet Union was the fact that many of the country's former republics possessed nuclear weapons—hundreds of tons of nuclear weapons material were spread across numerous sites in Russia and other former Soviet states. Not only was there a concern that these republics might use the weapons for their own—potentially misguided—purposes, but there was an even more urgent concern that some weapons might be sold to rogue states, such as North Korea, Iraq, and Iran, or find their way into the hands of terrorist groups.

As a result, Russia asked the United States for cooperation in securing these weapons and the materials that were used to build them. In 1991, the Congress passed the Nunn-Lugar Act, which led to development of the Nunn-Lugar Cooperative Threat Reduction Program—a collaborative effort between the DOD and Russia's Ministry of Defense for the denuclearization of the former Soviet republics.

However, DOD was not adequately staffed to do all of its work on this program. The DOD therefore hired contractors to help safeguard the designated nuclear weapons. With its long history of work for the Defense Nuclear Agency, the Department of Energy, Los Alamos, and the other national labs, SAIC seemed to be a perfect choice to help. SAIC was awarded contracts to develop high-level technical and administrative plans for a variety of contractors to secure and clean up the related materials, including deactivating and moving warheads, destroying missiles, and disposing of rocket fuel using environmentally proper methods.

This work demonstrated that despite the end of the Cold War, there were plenty of potential enemies in the world, and that our nation would need to remain vigilant to counter them. And while budgets would shrink in SAIC's traditional areas of expertise, other budgets would grow as we faced these new threats and prepared to deal with them. SAIC understood this shifting of priorities, and continued—and grew—its close partnership with the federal government in the years to come. At the same time, the company continued to diversify its business into commercial and international markets. This diversity in markets and competencies in a rapidly changing world helped SAIC to thrive. Events such as the end of the Cold War; the terrorist attacks of September 11, 2001; and the governance failures of Enron, Arthur Anderson, and Worldcom all had an impact on SAIC. If it had not been for the diversity of SAIC's presence in many government, commercial, and international markets, the impact of market changes could have proved fatal, as it did for many other companies.

13

The Challenge: Governance— Sustainability or Transition?

SAIC is a truly unique company—probably the only company of its size that is so thoroughly owned and controlled by its employees and so thoroughly dedicated to national interests. The success we have enjoyed over the last several years has been due to our employee ownership and policy setting philosophy, along with lots of dedication and hard work from everyone in the company. It is vital that the decision process of maintaining sensible, not short-term goals remain[s] within SAIC. It will take everybody's understanding of what the company is about to continue that process.

—from *Principles and Practices of SAIC*

Few corporations have had a board of directors as unique and far-reaching as the one that governed SAIC over the company's more than 35 years of existence. With a mix of SAIC top executives, high-ranking former government and military brass, including former Secretaries of Defense Melvin Laird and William Perry, and former National Security Agency Director

Admiral Bobby Inman, industry leaders, academics, and other professionals, such as former Scripps Institute of Oceanography director Ed Frieman and University of Virginia engineering professor Anita Jones, the members of SAIC's board have been well qualified for the job.

WHY HAVE A BOARD ANYWAY?

While corporations are designed to be governed by boards of directors, what is a board's real purpose and who should be on it? Is the reason for having a board of directors to try to maintain the status quo—acting as a conservator of a company's core values—or to help grow the organization? Or is it some combination of both?

Governance was not a common word in my vocabulary for much of the company's history. In keeping with my openness to new ideas, I felt that—aside from high ethical standards—our board should not follow rules developed by business schools as guidance for public companies. Regardless of our size we were, after all, a privately held company—subject to strict laws—but not subject to the same laws as public or regulated companies.

My point of view was that SAIC's board should ideally fulfill four primary objectives beyond their standard governance roles in the areas of management, fiduciary oversight, and business strategy. In my estimation, the first—and perhaps most important—objective was to protect the company's unique employee-ownership culture. The second objective was to bring top people into our management team with experience operating other high-tech companies—men and women who could help build SAIC. The third objective was to work to recruit other board members—especially those who could help the company win business and acquire senior management employees. The fourth and final primary objective for the board was to help with succession planning. While the extent to which these objectives were achieved over the years can be debated, what cannot be debated is the fact that SAIC's board played a very major role in shaping the company into what it is today.

I was a fan of large boards—after all, they were consistent with my "none of us is as smart as all of us" philosophy. At one point, we had something like 22 directors on the board. Throughout the first couple of decades, the board was mostly comprised of a 50:50 mix of SAIC senior executives (inside directors) and influential business and former federal government and military leaders (outside directors). The inside directors brought with them an intimate knowledge of how the company worked, its customers, its employees, and its strengths and weaknesses. The outside directors brought with them a big-picture perspective unmatched by the inside directors, as well as a variety of contacts—both in and out of the government. The outside directors could be very helpful in terms of providing insight into where the markets were going (which then helped drive the company's investment strategy), what sort of people to hire, and what customers to approach with proposals.

In addition to the regular meetings of the full board of directors, there were also a wide variety of board committees—more than similar companies would typically have.

First, there were the traditional committees such as compensation and audit. According to former SAIC executive and board member John Glancy, however, even the traditional committees were used in a different way than most companies used them. Says Glancy:

> Our Audit Committee has always been very active—it got down into detailed operations of the company. Bob Beyster actually used the Audit Committee to ferret out and identify issues that the company should be dealing with to make sure they were being taken care of. I don't think audit committees in other companies typically worked that way, at least until Sarbanes-Oxley. Now, of course, they are much more active. But we were active from the very beginning.

Second, the range and number—up to a dozen in its heyday—of board committees was unconventional in the industry. There were nontraditional board committees for stock policy, environmental, health, energy, and international. The International Business Committee played an important role in convincing me that SAIC should be doing international work.

The board was very much involved in the acquisition process. Although board approval was not necessary when SAIC purchased Network Solutions for about $5 million in 1995—my own authority covered that amount—the members were very much aware of the deal. There were very few cases where an acquisition would be approved by the board's executive committee or me that the entire board was not totally informed before the deal was done. The board did weigh into the process when SAIC's executive team decided to approach Bellcore—resulting in a $640 million acquisition, by far the largest one in the company's history up to that point. Even though many of the company's acquisitions could be approved by the executive committee or by me, the full board was informed in advance and the members could have intervened if they wanted to.

BOARD COMMITTEES

SAIC's board of directors chartered numerous committees for a variety of different purposes. While the committees changed somewhat over time, the following list is representative:

- *Executive Committee* took action on behalf of the board of directors during intervals between regularly scheduled board meetings, and oversaw and assisted in the formulation and implementation of human resource management, scientific research policies, and financial matters.

- *Compensation Committee* approved the salaries of the CEO and all executive officers, approved compensation contracts or severance packages for executive officers, established objective performance goals for executive officers under SAIC's bonus compensation plan, determined the amounts to be paid if these goals were satisfied, and issued reports to the Securities and Exchange Commission (SEC) regarding compensation policies for the CEO and the four other most highly compensated executive officers.

- *Operating Committee* approved offers by SAIC to sell shares of Class A stock, approved contracts, approved amendments to the employee benefit and incentive compensation plans, authorized filing of registration statements and reports with the SEC, called the annual meeting of stockholders, reviewed preliminary agendas for meetings of the board, adopted supplemental resolutions, and authorized mergers and acquisitions.

- *Audit Committee* provided oversight responsibilities related to the integrity of SAIC's financial statements, compliance with legal and regulatory requirements, the independent accountant's qualifications and independence, and performance of the company's internal audit function and independent accountants.

- *Nominating Committee* established a procedure for identifying nominees for the board of directors, reviewed and recommended to the board criteria for board membership, and proposed nominees to fill board vacancies as they occurred.

- *Technical Advisory Group* (known internally as the Brown Panel) was composed of SAIC board members and selected eminent outside technical consultants. Its job was to keep the company abreast of the very latest developments in technology and policy on a worldwide basis.

- *Board Ethics Committee* oversaw company ethics issues, maintaining a hotline that was monitored carefully and taking referrals from the Employee Ethics Committee in cases that could not be resolved or properly dealt with at a lower level of the organization. The committee also took up ethics questions and issues that were otherwise worthy of attention at the company's highest level.

- *Stock Policy Committee* engaged specialists on stock structure to work on improving SAIC's stock system and stayed aware of changing laws and regulations affecting employee stock ownership plans. It also set the company's quarterly stock price.

- *International Business Committee* recommended international objectives, policies, and procedures to the corporation's management team, and it reviewed relationships and assessed potential risks in international transactions. All new proposals for international business were required to be approved by this committee.

THE IMPACTS OF SARBANES-OXLEY AND OTHER GOVERNANCE CHALLENGES

For much of its existence, SAIC's board acted as a consultative body to help the company's top management team and me review business practices—including stock systems and price—and to identify and track emerging business opportunities and markets. Board members performed these duties either through their own contacts or knowledge, or by chartering management committees to monitor specific areas of interest and then periodically report their findings back to the board.

For example, the Technical Advisory Group (Brown Panel)—a group of very talented technical people, headed by former Secretary of Defense Harold Brown, who met on a regular basis—kept a very close eye on emerging trends in key markets, including defense, national security, information technology, and more. This committee made recommendations to the board on where the company should focus its resources, including specific proposal opportunities or acquisitions.

According to Admiral Bobby Inman, my influence was strongly felt by the board. Says Inman:

> There was a board of directors, but there wasn't much doubt—certainly, in the early years—that Bob Beyster ran the company. The board did pretty much what Bob Beyster thought was right. The bulk of the board members were added for the perceived contributions they would make to SAIC. They did not always make those contributions. The primary vision came from Beyster, not the board.

However, later in the board's history—particularly after the turn of the century—the board began to take a more active and assertive role in corporate governance. Then, with the coming of Sarbanes-Oxley, the company had to devote more of its administrative time and attention to dealing with the fallout. Suddenly, there were all sorts of administrative tasks that the board decided to do which utilized large amounts of company resources. There was little wrong with that because SAIC had a number of systems that needed to be improved, but a big impact of Sarbanes-Oxley was to force the company to focus internally on its systems management. This caused the company to lose some emphasis on the outside—on our customers. Before Sarbanes-Oxley, we spent most of our time focused on our customers.

Bureaucracies begin from the assumption that many employees can't be trusted to do the right thing—thus, the need to have people to watch the workers, and then watchers to watch the watchers, and so on into paralysis. But for SAIC, the working assumption was that employees—given the objectives of the company—could be trusted to make logical decisions and exercise considerable authority in meeting those objectives.

Sarbanes-Oxley also starts with the assumption that many business leaders can't be trusted to do the right thing. Although there are always a few for whom this assumption is true, it is not valid for most of the business world. Most businesspeople are motivated by the desire to create jobs, meet their financial objectives, and make a positive contribution to society through the goods and services their companies offer. For this majority, aspects of Sarbanes-Oxley add a layer of bureaucracy, add costs and complexity to their operations, and provide questionable value added. Much of the corporate world tolerates institutional bureaucracy. At SAIC, we diligently minimized it.

" 'Season's Greetings' looks O.K. to me. Let's run it
by the legal department."

In his book *The Entrepreneurial Imperative,* Carl Schramm—president and CEO of the Ewing Marion Kauffman Foundation—makes a compelling argument that more legislation is not necessarily the best solution to corporate transgressions. Says Schramm:

> Bad judgment and misbehavior cannot be legislated out of existence. At some point, laws and regulations have only marginal, or zero, effect. As law professor Brett McDonnell wryly notes, "Ethics codes are nice, but of questionable importance. Ethical behavior is crucial; ethics codes, not so much. . . . Enron had a great code of ethics."[1]

It's important to remember that Sarbanes-Oxley and other recent legislative initiatives aimed at protecting employees and shareholders in U.S.-based companies are the result of the transgressions of just a handful of misgoverned companies. Good corporate governance can address these issues effectively without the need for intrusive regulatory oversight. Fortunately, Congress has become aware of some of the problems this legislation is causing, and is actively exploring changes for the better.

THE BOARD AS CONSERVATOR
OF CORE VALUES

I believe we did a good job of creating support for the employee owner-ship idea among the many SAIC employees and managers who liked our company culture. However, I did not do as good a job at the board level. Board members were chosen—as I already described—primarily to help with scientific and business judgments and identification of markets. However, more attention was necessary to make sure that board mem-bers were knowledgeable on the core values of SAIC's unique employee-ownership culture. This does not mean that the company lost its emphasis on employee ownership, just that employee ownership was not always as central as I would have liked in making decisions during my last years at SAIC.

One possible solution to the challenge of maintaining a company's unique employee ownership model over the long run would be to explicitly charge the board with responsibility for sustaining the company's core val-ues, cultural attributes, and operating philosophies. This might most eas-ily be accomplished by establishing a management committee specifically chartered by the board's bylaws to do this—to promulgate its core values, cultural attributes, and business approaches emanating from employee ownership, and to sustain the employee-ownership model.

Early on I was concerned whether we could build an employee-owned corporation if we took it public through an initial public offering. Despite pressure to do so, I resisted this advice. As it turned out, the rapid growth of the company in size, employees, revenue, shareholder value, and profits gave us a lot of cushion to control our own destiny—especially given that we had little debt. Going public was not an absolute necessity in our first 35 years the way it became for some industrial companies that had large capital investments to make.

Further, I was not aware of many public companies that established employee ownership and maintained it. This made me very cautious on this score, especially because I had come to believe that our employees valued employee ownership. I later became aware that some companies like Procter & Gamble had established employee ownership and profit sharing as far back as the 1880s and had maintained about 25 percent employee ownership and a strong emphasis on it for over a hundred years, but that this took constant focus. United Parcel Service (UPS) and

Parsons, a major engineering and construction firm, also have strong employee ownership programs.

At times, I considered that going public and maintaining employee ownership might work, perhaps in a hybrid organizational structure. Maybe it would have made sense for me to work more closely with the board to manage this transition myself before retiring. That would have been quite an experiment indeed.

TURNING POINT: THE TECHNICAL ENVIRONMENT COMMITTEE

When we talk about corporate governance, we're generally focusing on the role that a company's board of directors plays in directing and controlling the organization. In most cases, a board of directors comprises both inside directors—often the CEO and top executives—and outside directors, who may be deeply experienced in the same industries in which the company does business. But where do regular employees—the men and women who get most of their companies' work done—fit into all this? Should they also play a role in the governance of the companies that they have dedicated themselves to? If so, what role should they play?

At SAIC, this role was fulfilled by the Technical Environment Committee (TEC), which established active communication links from SAIC's technical employees, management, and the board of directors. While some of the many committees in SAIC had only a minor impact on the company's day-to-day operations, others had a major impact. TEC was one of the committees that had a major impact on us, and I personally—along with the board of directors, and other top leaders in the company—listened to the TEC's advice and recommendations. I believe employees appreciated the fact that their voices were being heard at the top of the organization. The fact is that their opinions were heard, and their advice was often heeded.

Bill Scott—tapped by me to found and chair the influential TEC—was invited to attend SAIC board meetings as an observer representing the employees. How this committee came to be is a lesson in employee participation all by itself. Says Scott:

> In about 1979, when former Defense Secretary Melvin Laird joined the board, a number of employees were concerned that he wouldn't know anything about working conditions at SAIC, so we started talking about the need to have an employee on the board. One of the fellows—Charlie Hill out of Huntsville—got enough proxies together to elect an employee onto the board. Charlie brought the proxies to Dr. Beyster and explained that a number of us were concerned about the board being all these famous people and not representing us. Bob and Charlie negotiated and agreed to create a Technical Environment Committee. Somehow I was tapped to lead it.

The TEC became a very important avenue for employee participation within SAIC, providing both a way for employees to communicate their opinions, desires, and concerns to the board, and for the board to provide insight on leadership changes, big contract wins, ongoing challenges such as fast-rising health care costs, and much more. The committee allowed us to avoid the "us versus them" mentality that often divides companies, and all views—not just the views of a particular constituency—were brought forward to the board.

One contentious issue that the TEC had an impact on was health care benefits. During the 1980s, there was a substantial increase in medical care costs in the United States, and every business started to feel the pain as profits were squeezed. I felt strongly that we had to keep our costs competitive so that our customers would continue to award us contracts. As the costs continued to increase, however, it became increasingly difficult to keep our fringe benefits rate the same. We had a difficult job restructuring the benefits every year in order to maintain the same bidding rates and yet not be draconian in the benefit cuts that were required to accomplish that goal. It seemed like a no-win situation.

The TEC floated a new idea to the board—cancellation of the "top-hat" supplemental benefit, a special benefit plan that covered the cost of extra physicals and other medical procedures for our top management team. After discussing the issue, we agreed with the TEC's suggestion to cancel the benefit and used the extra cash to subsidize the premiums of the lowest-paid employees, on whom the increasing medical costs were having the greatest impact. The net result was that SAIC's lower-paid employees received a lower premium rate than everybody else—at zero cost impact on the company.

Through our experience with TEC and many other committees and employee forums, we learned how employee-owners can participate in their company and make a real difference in the decisions that are made—even by the board of directors. I won't say that having employees participate in governing SAIC was always an easy or a pleasant experience, but I will say that our company was the better for it.

14

The Future:
New Beginnings

The answer to the United States's competitiveness problem is not just giving employees a small piece of the company through a retirement plan. Nor is the answer just letting employees pick the color of their office. It is no one gesture. It is a package—a corporate culture that must be nurtured every day. One that supports the employee, motivates him or her to excel in their job, and rewards good work. This can be the answer to long-term growth, retaining employees, and increased productivity.[1]

—J. Robert Beyster

I am often asked my views on the future. What is the future of business, of employee ownership, of the great company that we built? What technologies show the most promise? Into which initiatives should leaders—corporate and government—direct their limited resources? I guess this is to be expected from someone who has spent so many years on this Earth and done so many different things. I grew up in an era that permits me to look at the world through a different lens than most people in the workforce today. I continue to keep in contact with many of my colleagues, recently through my blog, and I enjoy hearing and reading about the newest technologies—those just beginning to appear over the horizon—and then imagining how they will impact the country.

The question I am asked most often goes something like this: "Do you think a company like SAIC could be started up—and be successful over the long run—in today's business environment?" I do believe a company like SAIC could be established today. It would be different, however, since SAIC was established when the business environment was not the same. The government market when SAIC started was directly influenced by Vietnam and the Cold War. Technology in the commercial world was dominated by large industrial firms such as IBM, GE, and AT&T. The landscape has changed dramatically since then. Technology development has been pushed down to smaller, more entrepreneurial companies.

If I were to do it all over again, the company would still be employee owned and we would address nationally important programs in the federal marketplace, specifically, defense, energy, and counterterrorism. Initially, our approach to financing would be unlike that at SAIC, where we started small and bootstrapped our way. I am sure that today there is an abundance of private investors who would be interested in helping to finance such a company. In today's business environment, I would expect the company to grow slower than SAIC because SAIC entered the government and commercial marketplaces at a very opportune time.

I also often hear questions along the lines of: "Do you believe there is a future for employee ownership?" The global role of SAIC-style employee ownership is somewhat uncertain. Many vehicles exist to build mid-size and large employee-owned companies. For example, employee-owned companies can be built in a hybrid model combining leveraged employee stock ownership plans (ESOP) with direct ownership vehicles. This is being done successfully by a number of companies, for example, Alion Science and Technology of McLean, Virginia, and others.

I believe that the number of ESOP companies will probably remain about the same—about 12,000 or slightly more—and that they will continue to keep the enthusiasm going for employee ownership. Building largely directly owned companies like SAIC, however, will be challenged by the countervailing desire of many company founders and executives to hold ownership closely within a small group in hopes of cashing out for a large financial reward by way of an initial public offering or buyout. There are very few business schools today that specialize in educating students on the advantages of an employee-owned company (exceptions are the Beyster Institute at the Rady School of Management at the University of California, San Diego, and the School of Management and Labor Relations at Rutgers University), so when people who have a traditional business education are interested in building a company, they tend to proceed with the venture capital and public ownership route.

To make employee ownership an attractive system for businesses to adopt, government has to do its part, too. There are still those who oppose ESOP legislation—particularly certain business journalists—but so many benefits have come out of establishing them that it is important that Congress maintain this legislation in the future.

Another issue I'm often asked to comment on is America's competitive position. We read articles and books expressing concern about competition from Asian nations, particularly India and China. While there is some cause for concern about the displacement of American jobs to offshore companies, we have experienced offshore movement of U.S. manufacturing in the past. What we learned from this is that the U.S. industrial complex can retool to differentiate itself, becoming more productive and efficient, driving further economic growth. The development of the Internet and the associated information technology and infrastructure (Google, eBay, etc.) are examples of this. In order to continue to differentiate American industry in the future, we must continue to cultivate and foster entrepreneurial innovation.

David Gergen wrote an article—"Great to Good?"—that discusses business author Jim Collins' assertion that America is on the brink of going from great to good. This article raises interesting questions in my mind about the future competitiveness of the United States. I have always felt SAIC had a chance to improve that competitiveness—even in a small way—and that we should communicate this to others. I remember in the 1980s having a discussion with a high-level White House advisor to President Clinton and a member of the Council on Competitiveness who felt that employee ownership could not have any impact whatsoever on U.S. competitiveness. I disagreed at the time and still disagree with this viewpoint. The traditional American strengths of innovation and entrepreneurial vigor continue to provide significant advantages in the competition to develop and market new technologies. However, to be competitive over the long run, companies must reinforce these strengths with flexible organizational structures that give employees the freedom to make suggestions and have a real impact on day-to-day operations. Employee ownership is just one response to the challenge of improving American competitiveness, but one that creates the right environment for changes to flourish.

It is clear to me that American businesses must look internally to find better ways to compete in today's marketplace. It is not realistic to believe that tomorrow's public and private companies will immediately become employee owned. Change is painfully slow. But I am a strong believer in the power of the masses (for an interesting perspective on this power, read *The Wisdom of Crowds* by James Surowiecki). I believe in grassroots movements for change and that each person in each organization bears a responsibility that can affect the competitiveness and security of the country. In addition, there are many organizations doing positive things, for example, the Ernst & Young Entrepreneur of the Year awards program.

The advancement of our educational system will need to contribute to our economic growth through the training and support of more science and engineering educators and curriculum development is critical. However, this will not happen on its own. Our business leaders at all levels are responsible for fostering the development of a competitive and technically trained workforce by funding university programs in science and engineering.

Finally, we must recognize that we are in danger of drowning American business—and choking off the creativity of our enterprises—in a sea of restrictive legislation. Anti-business legislation—while possibly well intended—may serve to protect uninvolved shareholders of public companies from injury. Worse, overly restrictive legislation threatens to curtail the creativity and innovation that have made America great. I am pleased that Congress and the Securities and Exchange Commission are actively trying to correct this overkill. Otherwise, this situation could force entrepreneurs to make choices that are not in their best interests or that of our country. I'm hoping at a minimum, Congress will boil down such legislation to the essentials.

Our legislators should focus their attention on the underlying problems which lead to corporate governance abuse. The ethical failures and lack of corporate director accountability to management, employees, and shareholders may represent the greatest of all threats to American business. This has been demonstrated by the recent corporate governance failures at Hewlett Packard which led to board and management resignations. Legislation that protects employees and shareholders from ethics and governance abuses and forces corporate directors to become more involved in the success of their companies would be more productive.

I am often asked what I consider to be the most important technology trends to watch in the future. There are at least three that merit particular attention. One thing to keep in mind is that key technology areas don't change suddenly. For example, SAIC has been in the counterterrorism business for decades, yet this will be more important in our future than ever before. Whether you agree with the items I have selected or not, I can guarantee that each will have a significant impact on our lives and that they should be considered in serious business-planning exercises.

One critical area is warfighting—specifically, future combat systems and counterterrorism. Future combat systems need to be designed for the new threats. They should be mobile, semiautonomous, and laden with advanced communications technology. The Defense Advanced Research Projects Agency (DARPA) and the military services are today funding research and demonstration projects in this and related areas. One such area is robotics. The promise of robotics has been recently demonstrated by DARPA's Grand Challenge program in which competing teams assembled autonomous vehicles that successfully drove more than 100 miles across the desert—avoiding obstacles along the way—with no human intervention.

Today we are fighting against an enemy that doesn't have the same values system we have and this war will not soon end. In the Middle East, significant conflicts have gone on for centuries, long before the September 11, 2001, attacks on the World Trade Center and the Pentagon. We are not accustomed to long-term conflicts—we don't work well in that environment. Terrorism has got to be dealt with before we can efficiently focus our efforts on the future. The necessary share of our resources—diplomatic included—should be put into trying to get this endemic problem better under control.

For example, one of our most serious threats arises from improvised explosive devices (IEDs). Putting together the technical advances we are making in microcircuits and miniaturization, with sensor systems and robotics that can detect, monitor, and destroy IEDs, should be and is today a national priority. Many techniques have been tested to identify and neutralize IEDs—and there is progress—but to date no systems solution.

Ultimately, our technology investments in counterterrorism have been only partially effective in detecting explosive materials (e.g., gels/liquids) on commercial airplanes. It is the awareness and identification of those who mean us harm that warrants our investment. The development of biometric technologies for identification and authentication (e.g., fingerprint readers, iris scanners) and the wireless tagging of authorized personnel and equipment is a promising approach. We should use technology to our benefit without compromising personal privacy.

A second critical area is energy, including alternative energy. Conservation—both in the energy and transportation sectors—is a promising solution, but it unfortunately does not solve all of the needs. In these days of relatively cheap oil and gas, there is little incentive for users to conserve or for oil companies to explore for more resources. Greatly improved fuel economy standards and a shift toward biofuels (cellulose based biomass that can be refined into ethanol and other fuels) are two approaches for reducing our dependence on foreign oil. At $50 to $60 a barrel, coal liquefaction becomes viable and projects are in the planning phase. Oil shale is probably 20 years away due to serious environmental and water resource constraints.

I do not think that using hydrogen as a fuel makes much sense today. Hydrogen gas does not occur naturally—it takes energy to produce, which currently requires fossil fuels. And there still remains the considerable challenge of storage, transport, and safety of hydrogen, which cannot today be easily answered.* We have an abundance of fossil fuels, as does China. We should be working on ways to burn these fuels with minimal emissions and impact from carbon dioxide (CO_2). Carbon sequestration and energy storage that will make renewables more appealing and reliable should be a priority of our government research.

The hybrid car is probably a good idea to help conserve fossil fuels for the short term. The Japanese have led the way so far, but both Ford and General Motors are getting seriously involved. U.S. automakers won't rectify their profitability problems until they adopt these newer technologies and regain market share.

Nuclear fusion power generation has been a costly disappointment. The devices to produce fusion are so large and take so much energy that there is little hope for it in this century. I have a feeling that we may get desperate enough in this nation that nuclear reactors will be looked at more favorably soon. What happens when a barrel of oil costs $100? We may have to accelerate our action on these other energy sources. The latest nuclear power reactors are much safer than earlier versions, and technology is offering new innovations such as proliferation-resistant fuels and processes. I feel that commercial and federal government research programs have not addressed these problems adequately over the past many years, at least partly because of the low cost of oil. If the government could create a DARPA-like energy program, we might get closer to solving many of our energy problems. It is rumored that Congress is considering establishing such a program now.

A third national priority is the environment. Now that most experts (including President George W. Bush) agree we are faced with global warming, what should our response be, and where are the opportunities? The Pew Center on Global Climate Change has developed an agenda for a "Responsible Course of Action" to address climate change. Although I question some

---

* However, innovative automobile companies—including GM, Honda, and BMW—are working hard to address these issues.

of the recommendations, I particularly like their ideas for developing and implementing a program for trading carbon credits and tracking greenhouse gases, reducing energy consumption through policies that spur efficiencies, and participating in negotiations to establish combined emissions standards.

Al Gore reports in his book *An Inconvenient Truth* (Rodale, 2006) that an already existing body of affordable technology can bring U.S. carbon emissions down to below-1970 levels. These six steps include:

1. Reduction from more efficient use of electricity in heating and cooling systems, lighting, appliances, and electronic equipment.

2. Reduction from end-use efficiency, meaning that we design buildings and businesses to use far less energy than they currently do.

3. Reduction from increased vehicle efficiency by manufacturing cars that run on less gas and putting more hybrid and fuel-cell cars on the roads.

4. Reduction from making other changes in transport efficiency, such as designing cities and towns to have better mass transit systems and building heavy trucks that have greater fuel efficiency.

5. Reduction from increased reliance on renewable energy technologies that already exist, such as wind and biofuels.

6. Reduction from the capture and storage of excess carbon from power plants and industrial activities.[2]

A particularly attractive additional area of research for technologists is nanotechnology. The United Nations Millennium Report Task Force on Science, Technology, and Innovation states that nanotechnology will be very important for sustainable development efforts in water, energy, and air pollution.

Another report—from the National Renewable Energy Library (NREL)—states that nanotechnology has the potential to double the efficiency of solar energy conversion to electricity. There are some contrary views on this matter from the toxic health standpoint, but this technology holds too much promise to be ignored. Although not discussed in NREL's report, there are other important fossil fuel technologies, such as tar sands, natural gas distribution, and clean coal that merit both federal and commercial investment. The known reserves of these fossil fuels are extensive and should continue to be developed, keeping emissions considerations in mind.

Promoting energy efficiency is a near-term way to address global climate change. It is key not only because of the cost and pollution reduction benefits, but also because it empowers consumers to deploy more options, often using cleaner energy. Utility companies are struggling to deliver renewable power generation because of the traditional way that they serve the market. By integrating solar with battery backup power at the retail and home level, the consumer can help reduce the peak load on the grid and increase reliability. Managing a highly decentralized electrical sector is difficult, but so is trying to maintain an aging power infrastructure.

We aren't going to solve these environmental problems without addressing them soon. This includes finding viable solutions for the physical security of our supply chains.

Beyond these specific areas of interest, American industry also has to be alert for and willing to take on challenges for the national good that are perhaps not in their realm of business. As one small example, in 1983, SAIC didn't know much about the America's Cup or 12-meter boat racing. The Australians had taken the America's Cup away from us, and to us at SAIC that indicated a failure of American technology in a world forum. Dennis Conner was having trouble finding people to rally around him and help him design a boat that could recapture the Cup. We looked within our company and found many sailing enthusiasts and experts who thought we should help. We were able to forge a winning technical team that helped bring home the Cup in 1987. That action was not intended to boost SAIC, but it did in many ways. I use this example to show that you can accomplish just about anything in this country if you set your mind to it and work hard enough.

In summary, to maintain our competitive and entrepreneurial leadership position among our global peers, American business leaders must assume responsibility with the support of our political leaders to foster innovation and commercial risk taking, which is the basis for our national economy. Many entrepreneurial companies, like SAIC, have the opportunity to lead the way for our nation. If we can maintain our focus on the proper education of our youth, the ethical and responsible corporate governance of industry, the empowerment of our workforce together with some form of equity sharing, and the development of the right technologies, we will continue the tradition of American commercial superiority and success.

Epilogue

Many books have been written—pro and con—on employee ownership. This book addresses one man's approach to building a large, employee-owned company from scratch. I thought employee ownership was the fair way to do things. Although it's not the standard business school recipe for building a company, I decided to stick with it and hoped it would produce a better work environment for the employees—and better products for the customers. I believe we accomplished both of those goals.

To excel in business, it is important for leaders to understand something about how their individual cognitive powers work. I never thought much about that in my 80+ years but, since my retirement, I have had time to ponder these matters. I now realize that, as a CEO, I paid too much attention to technical detail at the expense of process improvement for the overall business.

To succeed, leaders also need the ability to communicate and present their business cases convincingly to a wide assortment of people, including customers, employees, their boards, and financial and other business associates. Leaders must work hard and persevere through tough times. They must focus and not let their resources be diluted.

I am a bricklayer—I like to see something grow from nothing. I am a person who needs to be around people with whom I am comfortable. I am also driven to make decisions to get things done—not just talk about doing something. My head works better working with others, having produced many good ideas while in sessions with my peers and while running with them during lunchtime.

When SAIC started to grow, I really thought employee ownership would sweep the world. Unfortunately, most companies—especially those outside the United States and the United Kingdom—are not ready for it. Nevertheless, for many companies, employee ownership has worked well. It will take effort, but if you feel so inclined, I recommend you give it a try.

Better to try and then stop a program that's not meeting expectations than to anticipate failure and not try at all. One person can make a difference in a company—don't make the mistake of underestimating the importance of each person in your organization.

I pass these thoughts along (late in my life) in the hope that I may convince others to consciously identify those people, projects, and subject areas that they enjoy the most, and focus and participate in them early in life. I'm a curious person who is easily distracted, but I am sure if I had recognized my behavioral patterns earlier, I would have lived my life differently, focusing more narrowly on fewer areas of interest where I could have productively excelled. I am convinced, however, that the most worthless thing anyone can do is to strive to make billions. After all, how much money can one person intelligently dispose of?

There are people I like and seek out and those I'm not comfortable with and subconsciously avoid. As I review this situation, I have to admit many times I have been most productive working with a friend I respect. Other times I have not spotted the flaw in a complex personality or listened enough to others who were trying to advise me. There could be all kinds of reasons for this behavior. Hence, it's good to work with smart, open-minded people—who can present a variety of viewpoints—you can trust and who will help guide your decisions.

I am, in addition to the above, a "gut feel" guy on decisions. I intuitively have feelings about what is going to work based on a foundation of facts and experience developed by applying the scientific method to business. The question is: How much information is enough and what kind do you need for each decision? For that reason, I have always welcomed the opportunity to ask many questions of others to supplement and correct my gut feeling. Questions have always been easy for me to generate. It also helps in solving complex problems to break the problem into pieces and solve the easy parts first. I learned that early in life and never regretted using that approach.

I am very proud that the company I founded in 1969 today has revenues in the neighborhood of $8 billion a year. I can't say that I ever imagined this possibility when we signed the lease for our first offices in McKellar Plaza in La Jolla many years ago. Remember, SAIC is not a traditional entrepreneurial company. In addition to the financial numbers, we measured success by asking, "Did we accomplish what we set out to do?" and "Are we making an important difference?" In each case, I think we did. SAIC provided a good work environment. Employees had the freedom to pursue their business interests, as long as they eventually helped us build the company. They were given responsibility and control over their workspace, asked to help improve the company, and rewarded with ownership or the right to purchase stock based on their performance. That ownership value has increased through SAIC's success. And it has made a huge difference for our many customers, government as well as commercial.

As I mentioned in the Preface to this book, I kept my "None of us is as smart as all of us" poster close at hand throughout my years at SAIC. No matter which office I moved into—and there were many—that poster went with me, and hung above my desk. To me, these 10 little words mean seeking opinions of other key people in the company since it is easy to overlook some important point of view. I have tried to be all-inclusive and have ended up spending a great deal of time with a wide spectrum of knowledgeable people in the decision process. I'm sure we made better decisions because of it. In addition, seeking other opinions has been enjoyable for me to do. I would recommend using this technique in your decision process as well.

It is my hope that in reading this book, you have learned something new that will make your business better, more effective, and more productive. I encourage you to seek information regarding the various forms of employee ownership and participation. If you're starting a new company—or running one that is already well established—it is important to begin thinking of your company in the long term, and to share the wealth with those who are helping you and not just view them as employees. Employee ownership will help you hang on to good employees, be innovative, and be more productive. You don't need miracles, just small steps forward.

I learned many lessons in the living business laboratory we called SAIC, and I continue to learn new ones every day. My legacy to SAIC's employees was a way of thinking about what is fair across the board in our technical community, including what is fair to the customer, employees, and stakeholders. That thinking has been focused on understanding equity sharing in SAIC, not as an entitlement, but rather as a right to the fair portion of corporate equity that the employees themselves earned. I believe I left SAIC with a precious thing. SAIC is a peek into a vision of unselfish corporate ownership, not fully developed as yet, but worthy of further attention.

Starting and building SAIC was, along with the many good times I've shared with family and friends, the most fulfilling experience of my life. If you are ever fortunate enough to experience this same sense of fulfillment that comes from turning a vision into reality, then you will be a lucky person indeed.

About the Foundation for Enterprise Development

The Foundation for Enterprise Development (FED) was established in La Jolla, California, in 1986 by Dr. J. Robert Beyster with a broad charter to help develop successful enterprises in the United States and around the world. To accomplish this, over the past 20 years FED has focused on advancing entrepreneurship and employee ownership through its work with technologists, entrepreneurs, executives, governments, and educators in more than 40 countries.

In 2002, FED created and launched the Beyster Institute to focus on training, education, and consulting in employee ownership and entrepreneurship in the United States and worldwide. In 2004, the Beyster Institute became part of the Rady School of Management at the University of California, San Diego. The Institute actively assists individual companies in creating or enhancing employee ownership programs, and it has been widely recognized for its success in promoting entrepreneurship and regional economic development in the Middle East, North Africa, Russia, Central Asia, Latin America, and other emerging areas.

FED, as a private operating foundation, seeks to foster innovative scientific and technology companies and the promotion of free enterprise, primarily within the United States. To these ends, FED initiates and supports research, thought leadership, and education that advances and transfers the key principles and practices successfully used to grow SAIC to future generations of technical leaders.

It was Dr. Beyster's dedication to employing innovative science and technology to solve problems of national and global importance—and sharing the wealth with those who help build the company—that led, in part, to the tremendous success of SAIC. His commercial success and philanthropic ideals have produced an impressive model that FED seeks to disseminate and propagate through its grants and research, education, and consulting programs.

Appendix A

My Life
before SAIC

E very leader is unique, reflecting at any particular moment the sum of his or her experiences to that point. I am no different; my actions, perspectives, and philosophy as CEO and board chairman of SAIC were directly influenced by key events in my life before SAIC—from a few years after my birth until my last day with General Atomic. Here is a brief recounting of these key events.

THE BEGINNING

I was born in Detroit, Michigan, in 1924, and I spent my early days in a rented duplex flat on Ferndale Avenue in Detroit. My grandparents lived in the unit downstairs, and they were to have a big impact on my life. My grandmother loved to make me happy, and I loved her for that, but my grandfather had a vicious temper and he was hard on both my mother and my grandmother. In those days when road rage had not yet been defined, he loved to roll down his car window and scream at other drivers.

In 1929, during the Great Depression, my grandfather just managed to make ends meet—as a salesman of some sort. My grandmother was a housewife and extremely thrifty. The net environment to which I was exposed was cramped, dark, and full of fear of my grandfather and father's bad moods and temper tantrums. There was always a lot of tension in the air. But my grandmother and mother protected and worried endlessly about me—that never stopped.

Family origins were very much a topic of conversation in Michigan in those days, and I was exposed to many ethnic remarks. My father was of French and Dutch origin and my mother was French and German. My father's family was well to do but thrifty, and my mother's family was lower middle class. Religion was a major point of contention in my family because my dad's family (Beyster) was Presbyterian, and my mom's family (Jondros) was Catholic. My mother insisted that I be baptized a Catholic—this was a time when it made a huge difference to others which church you attended, and where you were going to end up after you died (heaven or hell, or possibly purgatory). My mother was slightly resented by the Beyster clan since they generally looked down on Catholics. That didn't extend to me—I was treated well for some reason.

GROSSE ILE, MICHIGAN

When I was five (1929), we moved into a beautiful new house on Grosse Ile, Michigan. My father was a general contractor, and he had a partner named Olmstead, who wasn't very careful with house plans and budgets. Despite flunking out of the University of Michigan engineering school, my father designed beautiful mansions for some of the richest men in Detroit, if not the world at that time. His partnership was quite successful until later in 1929 as the Depression worsened. Our new house wasn't a mansion, but it had four bedrooms and was built from the very best materials.

Grosse Ile had a mix of economic brackets, from poor working class to the ultra-rich automotive executives. The Beyster name was synonymous with success, and it opened doors to many construction jobs in the Detroit area. My father's business offices were in the General Motors building and then the new Fisher building. My father took me to these offices quite often, and I saw the wealthy business part of Detroit in full motion. The energy and enthusiasm of these folks was contagious, and I wanted to grow up to be as successful as they were. My mother pushed me to aspire to be president of the United States, and I daydreamed about the possibility.

Toward the end of 1929, the Depression began to deepen. Due to poor investments by Mr. Olmstead, Beyster and Olmstead Incorporated depleted its design business and had to be cut way back. Companies and banks were going bankrupt all over Detroit, but Grandfather Beyster would not let that happen to my father. The successful Beyster Lumber Company (located under the Ambassador Bridge in Detroit) would help maintain financial credibility for my father during these dark times. My father was able to keep his contractor's license and an office in Detroit doing design and construction supervision jobs that other Beyster family members helped him find.

This whole series of events had a lasting lifelong effect on me. I saw mansion after mansion boarded up on Grosse Ile as their owners went bankrupt due to their now worthless investments. It was during this time that I had it drummed into me how bad bankruptcy was—no self-respecting person would ever do it. The source of this deathly fear of bankruptcy still resides within me, so I have been careful in SAIC to fully understand the financial deals in which we were involved.

After a few years, my uncle Harold Foss got my father a new job at the Ternstead Corporation, a car trim subsidiary of General Motors on Fort Street, despite the fact that jobs were very scarce for noncollege-degreed industrial engineers. Under my father's influence, I developed an unswerving belief that General Motors was the greatest and most successful company in the world, Detroit the greatest city, and the University of Michigan the greatest university. Buying a non-GM car (or, heaven forbid, a foreign car) was antithetical to these beliefs, and a definite "no-no." If it hadn't been for SAIC's involvement with Ford Motor Company sponsoring the America's Cup event in 1987, I would never have bought a non-GM car.

My schooling at Grosse Ile started in grade school and ran through ninth grade. My mother—who was very worried about my getting a good education—was unimpressed with the Grosse Ile school system and saved enough money from my father's smallish salary at Ternstead to send me to high school in neighboring Trenton, Michigan.

Summers on Grosse Ile were especially lonely for me. I spent much of my time riding my bike to the large dirigible hanger to view the proceedings there and trying to get myself invited to swim in the Knudsen swimming pool. William Knudsen was president of General Motors at the time. Only twice—during my adolescence—did I go to summer camp. We learned to swim and canoe at camp, and I found out there that I was not good at many sports. To compensate, I always tried harder. I became very interested in scouting, eventually earning the rank of Star Scout.

I spent three of my final high school years at the Trenton Slocum Truax High School where I participated in track and debate, which helped keep me busy. I was class salutatorian at the end of my senior year and gave a commencement talk on the theme of "Excelsior." The point of the talk was that graduates need to try hard to excel in whatever occupation we chose to undertake and avoid underestimating what we are capable of—advice that I would take to heart as I embarked on my career.

U.S. NAVY

World War II began as I finished high school, so—like so many of my peers—I enlisted in the military, choosing to join the U.S. Navy. The Navy was planning for a long war and decided to bulk up its officer corps. I, along with many of my schoolmates were tested and the Navy decided to put me through college under its V-12 program, which paid all of my expenses at the University of Michigan. The GI Bill provided support after the Navy V-12 program ran its course. I graduated with majors in math and physics, and that's something I probably never would have done without the U.S. Navy. They made that decision for me. I had been headed in other directions.

I had a short tour on a destroyer on the East Coast. When the war ended, the Navy was overstaffed with ensigns, so they put me on inactive duty and I didn't really know what to do. I took some more tests, this time at the Johnson and O'Conner Institute in New York City. It was a good place to go for career aptitude testing. They gave me complicated 3D black blocks to put together and asked me to answer questions like, "What does this black spot look like?" At the end, they said, "Whatever you do, don't become a lawyer." Many times I have thought about how right they were. They said, "You seem to be going in the right direction, the Navy made a good decision for you in engineering and physics, so why don't you go back to school?"

And that's exactly what I did.

UNIVERSITY OF MICHIGAN

I went back to the University of Michigan, and I needed (no surprise) to earn money. I started working as a lab assistant in the university's physics department. Lucky for me I ran into a professor—Dr. Mark Wiedenbeck—who was looking for graduate student labor, and I worked very hard for him in his lab. He asked, "Why don't you get your PhD?" I thought, "That's the *last* thing I'd ever do—I don't want to be like *those* guys." But with his counsel and advice, which I needed many times in the late 1940s and early 1950s, I got through graduate school and obtained my PhD in physics.

At the time, this was the thing to do because nuclear energy was very much in vogue and many government and industrial organizations were doing remarkable research. Today, that would be a very questionable decision. But this was the 1940s, and the future of all things nuclear seemed very bright indeed, which led me to my next career destination.

LOS ALAMOS NATIONAL LABS

While most of my friends had gone directly from the University of Michigan to Los Alamos, New Mexico, home of the atomic bomb, I decided I would instead go to the Westinghouse Atomic Power Division to work on the nuclear submarine program. Unfortunately, I didn't like working there, so eight months after beginning my new career at Westinghouse, I made the move to Los Alamos where I was reunited with the rest of my University of Michigan colleagues. I was fortunate enough to get into the physics department there and work on some very large particle accelerators (Van de Graffs and cyclotrons), which I had enjoyed doing at the University of Michigan. I was very happy at Los Alamos, often working alone, or with one other person at most—usually either Martin Walt or Bob Carter.

At Los Alamos, I observed many entrepreneurs in action. There were researchers who would work at the lab for a while, get an idea, and then start a new company. That was very distasteful to me. I thought, "These scientists should be working on scientific projects, why are they worried about starting these crazy little companies?" It was a great time to be at Los Alamos—many of the scientists who had been there during the war returned, at least for a while. Hans Bethe—who was head of the Theoretical Physics Division at Los Alamos, and who went on to win the Nobel Prize in Physics in 1967—was one such person.

Although many of the scientists thought, "Bethe's a good physicist," they wanted to do their own projects. Thus, Bethe couldn't get anyone to assist on an experiment he wanted done, so I volunteered. I had admired him for years while in graduate school and figured anything he wanted done must be great. I worked very hard on that experiment and coauthored several publications with Bethe, which has never hurt me throughout my life. I also learned some physics and math from him, and I was an especially hard "theoretical physicist" to teach.

A branch point occurred at Los Alamos, because I could have been perfectly happy staying there and doing nuclear research. The lab had the facilities, the computers, and the associated software—everything a researcher needed. It seemed like paradise for a research guy. But many of my friends at the lab were leaving and going to a place called General Atomic (GA) in San Diego. On top of that, my wife wasn't too happy at Los Alamos, which had a profound impact on me. So I applied for a job at GA in San Diego. It just so happens that GA was interested in putting together an accelerator physics department at that time, so they hired me to do it.

This department was supposed to have an electron accelerator that would service the whole laboratory and be used by chemists, physicists, radiation effects people, X-ray spectroscopists, reactor people, and anyone else who needed our services. We bought three electronlinear accelerators, joined them together ourselves, and were able to enhance the machine to reach an energy of 100 million electron volts. GA ended up putting about $2 million into the facility, and DOD (Department of Defense) and AEC (Atomic Energy Commission) put in an equal amount.

I learned something in that process that would serve me very well in the future. I learned about corporate accounting and the other basics of building your own business. I enjoyed my position at GA, even though I complained a lot about little things. But then the research world changed rapidly, over just a few years. Large numbers of entrepreneurial people started leaving to start their own businesses. Again, entrepreneurship was not for me, it was too degrading.

My salary was decent at GA, and as long as I could do the kinds of research projects I wanted to do—including interesting contract research—why not stay there? By that time, there were 130 people working for me and we were pretty excited about what we had done with the linear accelerator we had put together. We worked on physics projects to understand the behavior of neutrons in power reactors as well as in nuclear weapons. I quickly learned about marketing, but unfortunately hadn't learned much about serious profit making.

I spent 12 years at GA but, as the environment changed, I became convinced I was not working on research of any great interest to the management of the company. GA's owners and management were interested in the large gas-cooled reactor business, not the experimental physics business. That research was okay to do, but it had to pay for itself. This was my first exposure to the cold realities of the private enterprise system.

This experience taught me a big lesson—that people should work for organizations in which management, particularly at the top of the organization, is interested in what you're doing, not just the bottom line. If they aren't interested in what you're doing, you shouldn't be there, even if you have a large investment in time and energy. If you stay, there will be constant tension, bickering, and conflict over differing objectives. It's good to evaluate every now and then. If top management doesn't have the same interests as you, then consider other options.

So it was for me the day I left General Atomic—at the age of 45 with a wife and three kids—to start my own company: Science Applications Incorporated.

Appendix B

SAIC Time Line

The following key events marked SAIC's progress from start-up to $8 billion science and engineering success story.

1960s	1970s	1980s	1990s	2000s
Key Programs				
BNL, LANL, AFWL, and DASA contracts to start nuclear weapons effect business	Strategic Air Command and Strategic Command programs initiated	Three Mile Island response; Radiation-monitoring business grows; VACIS cargo inspection developed	VACIS business formalized	Yucca Mountain radioactive waste management program award. Port security business expansion
	Royal Saudi Naval Forces Command & Control start; Naval engineering and systems work started	Strategic Defense Initiative Systems Architect is first complex (System of Systems) architect project	Desert Storm C4I support	9/11 response; Future Combat System contract; DHS base established; Army PM Guardian
	Software business entry with Safeguard Independent Verification & Validation	Army Missile Command contract; First FBI contract; America's Cup win using naval simulation models	Intelligence agency business established	Global Command and Control contract; Trilogy FBI contract; Defense Information Systems Agency Global Information Grid support
	National Institutes of Health entry with training & simulation; National Cancer Institute program work	Composite Health Care System first billion dollar award; Outsourcing IT with BP, Entergy, and San Diego County	National Cancer Institute Award: first Major GOCO setup	Pfizer IT migration award
	Business started in space and missile, energy and environment	Logistics business area established; first Office of Naval Research contract	Telecommunication and commercial business expansion	Utah Olympics: first major public security event

	1960s	1970s	1980s	1990s	2000s
Key Acquisitions/ Subsidiaries					
		ComSystems business created	Transcor acquired	Network Solutions, Inc. acquired	AmSec, LLC formed
		JRB Associates founded for non-DOD business	AmSec acquired	Bellcore acquired	Boeing Info Systems acquired
				PDVSA IT joint venture formed in Venezuela	Network Solutions sold; Telcordia sold
Size and Financial Milestones					
	Founded 1969 with three employees	$250k in revenues in FY1970	$150M revenue in FY1980	$1 billion in revenues in FY1990	$5.5 billion in revenue in FY2000
		20 employees	3,300 employees	11,500 employees	39,000 employees
			Co. 6 started for low rate structure	IDIQ contracts total $9 billion	
Key Employee Ownership					
		Direct stock purchases by key people	E.O. becomes institutionalized	IPO of NSI	"Retirement wave" begins
		ESPP started; Stock bonus plan (ERISA)	401K created; Technical Environment Committee created	First E.O. for Int'l. employees in PDVSA; Comprehensive stock program	
		Bull, Inc. founded	Bull, Inc. approved	Bull, Inc. improvements	Bull, Inc. dissolved

(continued)

	1960s	1970s	1980s	1990s	2000s
Key Employee Ownership *(Continued)*					
		Formula price developed; Outside appraisals for "fair market value"	Fight off attempts to create a public market in SAIC stock		SAIC's IPO
			The Foundation for Enterprise Development (FED) is founded		Beyster Institute founded and moved into UCSD
Management Processes					
		"Objectives and Strategy" developed	"Principles and Practices" developed; Corporate proposal center/PIE created	ISSAIC and web-based management information systems increase connectivity in SAIC	SOX implementation begins
		Brown Panel initiated	Business Acquisition Council established	Board International Business Committee and Risk Committee created	
		Meetings Week started	A-20 policy started for Firm Fixed-Price work	Atomic model introduced informally	
			Consolidation at Campus Point, California Headquarters	Experimented with various organizational structures to bring the breadth of SAIC to international and commercial business	

Appendix C

SAIC Principles
and Practices*

FOREWORD

The purpose of this paper is to provide a primer on the essential features of SAIC. Twelve important topics were chosen for discussion because our approaches to these particular matters have shaped the nature of the company. This document is meant for all in SAIC to read, think about, amend, question, and discuss openly. Hopefully, future revisions will state our beliefs even more clearly. Meanwhile this discussion should be used in explaining SAIC to interviewees and new employees because the company clearly has a different *modus operandi* than most of its competitors.

Another important reason for retabulating our basic tenets is that SAIC is being tested constantly by competitors who want our business, by the financial community to see whether we can be forced to do things we may not want to do at this stage, and by our customers who constantly compare our research efforts with those of other organizations. This process of testing the

---

*SAIC's *Principles and Practices* were written by J. Robert Beyster and originally published in 1987.

fiber of SAIC makes one wonder, at times, why we want to do things in a certain way when another way might be more expedient. This, then, is an attempt to discuss those things about which we all feel most strongly and which we want to be sure to preserve in the future.

GENERAL PRINCIPLES

SAIC is a company for professional people who want to perform superior scientific and technical work, who are willing to work hard to do it, who want to have a say in the policies and management of the company and feel that the company is their company, who want to be exposed to a minimal number of distracting outside influences and pressures, and who want to be fairly rewarded for doing good work both from a recognition standpoint and from a financial standpoint. It is not a get-rich-quick organization or a high-roller speculative organization. It is an organization where the long-term and short-term rewards are expected to be fair to all.

Integral to SAIC's success has been an uncompromising commitment to quality. A unique aspect of this quality stems from our long-term dedication to the promotion of national security. This includes support of government advisory panels and committees to contribute to the formulation of policies and strategies consistent with U.S. goals and capabilities. It also means striving to develop our business in projects that we wholeheartedly support as proper contributors to the national good.

It is also a tenet of SAIC that it be a national company working on important national issues and serving the nation through strategically placed, well-staffed offices. None of these offices are considered branch offices, and none of the people in these offices are considered field workers. Equality and informality should exist independent of location.

FREEDOM

SAIC has always provided its employees with more freedom to pursue their interests and professional careers than do most other companies. All parts of SAIC (even the more tightly managed entities) are far from the lockstep organizations with which we often find ourselves competing. Responsible individuals in the company use this freedom to conduct their business with a straightforward, generally decentralized approach to matters. Avoidance of strict conformity within SAIC has fostered the growth of one of the strongest professional staffs ever assembled in the United States.

With the most important characteristic of the organization, however, comes an individual responsibility that is equally important, namely, that no individual abuse the freedom in SAIC in a manner to cause risk to the company or to compete unfairly with associates. It is important to try to make clear to our employees (particularly the new employees), that how we get where we are going matters to us, that any route to the objective is not acceptable.

Most organizations have solved the problem of risk from individuals by severely curtailing freedoms. That is not SAIC's intention. Rather, we will continue to strive for a free and open company environment for the majority of our employees by limiting freedom of decision for those with poor judgment and by removing incurable cases. Moreover, because we are committed to minimizing administrative or technical bureaucracy, no one should be considered free from constructive criticism and the search for better ways to run our business.

It must be recognized that SAIC is a complex company. Although certain general points of view are set forth here, specific management actions may not always be in complete conformity, owing primarily to the very freedom of action we have been discussing. Thus, we see an organization, parts of which have different personalities. These personalities develop by mixing together the general ideals presented here, the management styles inherent in the various senior managers, the requirements imposed by the nature of our customers, and through experience.

QUALITY

Taking a long-term view of what is important for SAIC, the quality of our technical efforts must always come first. Not only those efforts on behalf of our customers, but also those using our own resources for internal research, in managing ourselves, and in performing all of our administrative and business functions. Our objective is to have the highest quality of people doing any professional job within the company and to be not only the best company around, but also a unique company in many customer business areas.

The quality control system which is now in place will be expected to enhance the high technical reputation the company already enjoys. Our quality control representatives (both group and corporate) will maintain continuous watch on current research to detect and correct work we cannot wholeheartedly endorse. The Executive Science and Technology Council will also participate actively in these efforts. Senior management personnel will consult frequently and regularly with this group to support its efforts.

GROWTH

Growth is necessary for maintaining the right working environment in SAIC. It provides opportunities for individuals to expand their technical areas of interest and to advance in management responsibility. Growth, of course, is also important in creating the financial rewards necessary to attract and hold the best people.

The company will endeavor to maintain overall annual revenue growth in the 15 percent to 30 percent range. Less growth would not provide career opportunities for our people and more growth might be impossible for us to manage consistently with other objectives. This growth will probably require a changing mix of large and small contracts, as well as improved success in winning competitive procurements in many business areas and much more work as a subcontractor to large prime contractors.

PROFIT

Our objective is that profits after tax should be in the 3 percent to 4 percent range. This is reasonable and sufficient to make SAIC an attractive investment to its employees and to provide the resources necessary to build the company—prime reasons why SAIC is not a nonprofit organization. The profits made over and above that objective can be invested in the company's people and its future. There are two "profit pools," one involving bonus rewards of stock or dollars to a wide range of people in the company (not focused on the few) and the other used to invest in projects to enhance the company's future.

STOCK

Employee ownership is the basic tenet for this organization and probably will continue to be. In keeping with this "employee-ownership" philosophy, SAIC is presently a nonpublic company and does not lend itself easily to becoming a public company. The basic premise of the SAIC stock policy is that those who contribute to the company should own it and that ownership should be proportional to that contribution and performance as much as feasible.

Being owned by employees allows us to do what we think is best for SAIC with a longer-term view and minimizes short-term pressures to compromise our goals and standards. To make this ownership philosophy work, SAIC has established a comprehensive stock program that includes all feasible methods for employee stock acquisition and permits liquidity to the stockholder on a fair basis. Thus, the customary investor motive of maximizing return on invested capital is replaced by a balanced set of motives combining financial reward, professional accomplishment, and independence.

INTERNAL INVESTMENTS

SAIC will carefully handle the funds available to invest in our future—both those that are covered by our normal reimbursable pools and those from profit. This means that we must be diverse in our approach to investment (including marketing) and not risk too much on any one thing. As should be expected, investment of pretax profits is heavily influenced by the Independent Research and Development Committee, which already has a well-established process for screening proposed IR&D investments. That committee, or an equivalent new one, will also review the capital expenditures in a similar way.

EXTERNAL INVESTMENTS

At the present time SAIC has cash reserves to invest in interest-bearing accounts, real estate, and/or selective acquisition. While most of this is currently invested in interest-bearing accounts, in the future real estate investments will become increasingly important, particularly those that could improve our annual overall financial performance. Although the necessary expertise to handle these complex matters is still developing, we must involve ourselves now in our real estate management.

Acquisition of other companies, particularly in hardware-related areas is an appealing possibility as a growth option. Other organizations our size are currently actively pursuing this conventional approach to growth. Our manufacturing, though of superior quality, is limited in type and quantity. Without de-emphasizing growth in studies and analysis, support services and system integration, we will consider strengthening our ability in the manufacturing area to increase diversity and take advantage of our present position.

Growth will be sought by internal expansion, by joint ventures with other manufacturers, and by acquisition of suitable small companies that strengthen both the engineering and production aspects of our manufacturing capability. Additional product lines are being sought for SAIT in particular, and perhaps other internal organizations as well.

The company systematically seeks potential acquisitions, and several are currently being evaluated. High-technology product lines under consideration emphasize communications and computer equipment. Other product lines are not excluded as long as they meet the test of compatibility with SAIC's business lines and overall philosophy.

SAIC's resources will be applied to acquisitions to the extent that they are not expended on IR&D, staff rewards, or real estate investments. It is not expected that acquisitions will be a primary contributor to the growth of the overall organization in the near future. In no case will any single investment, acquisition, or anything else be allowed to place the future of SAIC as a whole at risk.

PRODUCTIVITY

SAIC places a very high value on staff productivity. We have endeavored to maintain a reasonable cost structure and to make the best people possible available to the customer. Also, SAIC's organizational structure plays a key role in productivity by minimizing layers of management and decision making in order to focus on responding to its customers.

In keeping with this approach to being productive and responsive, we must give as much attention as possible to utilizing the best technology available. Applying the latest technology to communications, computer networking, conferencing, and building good financial reporting and management information systems enables us to further enhance our productivity.

A special challenge to an organization as far-flung as SAIC is to achieve the levels of coordination and cooperation needed for efficiency. As SAIC grows and the groups inevitably become more self-reliant, this challenge could become harder to meet. The Management Council, National Security Policy Group, regular gatherings of technical specialists, group meetings, and intergroup support on projects all provide for a healthy interchange of information. Each of these activities will be continued and strengthened. To encourage greater intergroup activity and to maximize the matching of talent and tasks, management personnel is expected to be aware of and provide for the use of resources company-wide wherever it makes sense. Corporate management personnel will be alert to and will promote intergroup support wherever it is feasible.

PEOPLE MANAGEMENT

SAIC is endeavoring to provide three parallel career paths, each of which is considered to be equivalent within the company: the technical path, the management/administrative path, and the marketing path. These paths can be combined to suit the interests of individuals and the company. Career opportunities must be equally appreciated in all three areas: management and marketing must not be the only paths recognized in terms of rewards.

If the company is to stay healthy, it must provide room for the regular advancement of deserving people. This is a principal consideration in making decisions about company growth. Career enhancement will be offered whenever possible. An example of how SAIC is making such provision is the Executive Science and Technology Council, which will both exploit the expertise of a select group of senior technical people and provide public recognition of their individual capabilities.

An organizational structure will be maintained to provide supervisory positions consistent with our focus on high technology and our desire to be responsive and flexible in dealing with our customers. SAIC recognizes the importance of training for people in leadership positions who, perhaps for the first time, are making decisions that have a direct impact on the people who work for them.

In addition to making positions for advancement available, we must provide the means for building individual reputations for technical excellence. The company strongly encourages the development and preparation of papers for presentation at professional meetings. The company also strongly encourages publication of papers and will provide a means for this.

Management and supervisory personnel are expected to be aware of the career opportunities, desires, and potential of their people. Further, they are expected to take an active part in shaping those careers. Moreover, as an equal opportunity employer, SAIC is dedicated to nondiscriminatory hiring and advancement practices.

Financial rewards at SAIC should be in the form of salary, bonuses, and/or stock. Salaries should be reasonable and appropriate to each individual within the company and bonuses and stock rewards should fit the excellence of the deeds performed.

Internal competition has always been a complex matter in SAIC, as it is in most companies in which aggressive, entrepreneurial people abound. Success through unfair competition and unfair tactics should not be rewarded at SAIC. That does not mean it has never happened, but it is not our policy. Success through cooperation, and through combining the best talents of our people, will be encouraged and rewarded.

In particular, as procurements grow in size, it is essential that we combine our best capabilities to win. In most instances, it is preferable for one group to take the lead and to accept the responsibility for making use of other resources in the company. Cooperation is also necessary in sharing limited support services and in being responsive to customer demands.

In essence, we expect our employees to treat each other in the same manner in which they would like to be treated. SAIC absolutely requires of its employees basic honesty in representing their work correctly, in any and all financial acts within the company, and in representing their individual credentials and past accomplishments. The integrity of the company is exemplified through the actions of all employees. Professional integrity is essential to fulfill contractual obligations, to maintain the quality of our products, and to uphold the reputation of SAIC. It grows within each individual's conscience and is fostered by maintaining a professional environment that tolerates only the highest quality output from each employee and thus the company as a whole.

Maintaining a professional environment must be our intent and must be reflected in the actions of all employees. It can only be achieved through leadership, example, and the constant awareness of the benefits of such an environment.

ORGANIZATIONAL STRUCTURE

The organizational structure that seems to fit SAIC best is one in which people who are interested in the same things work together. This occurs through general business area compatibility, a common customer base, or other factors. These factors important to our people and their customers combine to produce group organizational entities that are clearly not textbook in nature, but have proven over time to be viable from a financial, marketing, and a professional satisfaction standpoint. Therefore, SAIC's group structure will be allowed to evolve into the next phase of the company.

Financial and marketing considerations are also important determinants of the organization. Regional supervision is sometimes important and occasionally key individuals have served as organizational focal points within SAIC. All of the above notwithstanding, as opportunities to do so arise, SAIC management will attempt to combine, within the appropriate groups, people interested in similar business areas under managers with strong leadership ability.

Recognizing that as the company grows various business areas will fit different rate structures for selling our work, it is anticipated that a dynamic, flexible organization will continue to be necessary. A hard and fast, inviolate organizational structure with a fixed-block diagram will never fit the overall needs of SAIC. In keeping with this organizational concept, SAIC has successfully put in place a lean and sensible set of administrative procedures and signature authorities to control a very distributed operation. Furthermore, we believe that leaving as much autonomy at the operating level and providing as many discretionary resources as possible to those who generate them is the best approach for the long term.

MARKETING

How we go about our marketing is one of the most important considerations for the future of SAIC. Successful marketing is built primarily upon the reputation of the company and our technical staff for performing superior and, in some cases, unique technical work.

Since the primary operating entities within SAIC are the groups, most of the marketing resources should be left with them. Groups will continue to be organized around themes, and as much as possible, overlaps will be eliminated. Therefore, clear-cut marketing responsibilities will emerge in the groups as clear-cut themes develop.

It must be recognized by group and division managers that as they are given responsibilities for growth in specific business areas, their attention to planning this growth is absolutely essential. They are expected to use the best advice available in the company or elsewhere in their marketing strategies and to utilize the best technical talents in SAIC to complement their own staffs.

It is, of course, an interdisciplinary world in which we live, and so, major procurements generally involve many themes. The groups must, therefore, work together or with other companies where necessary to win. In such procurement efforts, Corporate must play a catalytic role: understanding what the groups do, bringing them together, picking the right leadership from a group, and encouraging the groups to extend their best efforts to do a good job of marketing together as a team. On large procurements, marketing is a team effort; there is nothing we can or should do to get around that. There has never been an occasion within SAIC where a number of people were not responsible for winning a large program.

As the company grows, it is to be expected that marketing will become more sophisticated in several areas, but the need to be concerned and serious about marketing will not change. The marketing information system is being developed to track the strategy of major procurements of interest to the company. In addition, complex issues relating to conflict-of-interest clauses in government procurements must be widely understood to enhance management decision making. Marketing resources should be carefully apportioned to those areas where a winning strategy is present—not an easy judgment. These resources (group and corporate) must also be carefully apportioned to maintain the company's high-technology base which has always been the foundation of the company and must not be lost in the process of growth. Finally, apportionment of marketing resources must also take into account the higher motives of helping the nation with issues of national security and of establishing SAIC as a nationally recognized asset with regard to research, strategic problems, and debate.

Marketing strategy, bid/no bid decisions, and understanding of past wins and losses are all in the developmental stages at SAIC, but their importance cannot be overemphasized. The example of how to go about doing this should be set by Corporate working closely with the rest of the organization.

PLANNING

Planning in SAIC is conducted in two related parts, operational planning and strategic planning. Operational planning is the process by which annual financial and qualitative objectives for each profit center and for the company as a whole are set. These objectives and standards, which are agreed upon early in the planning process, are also used in advanced rate negotiations with the government and they determine the size and structure of the corporate management and administrative organizations that must be put into operation early in the plan year. For these reasons, annual operating objectives and standards must be known, understood, and accepted throughout the company. They must be treated almost as moral obligations by managers and senior staff members, to be broken only in the most serious circumstances and then only with as much notice as possible.

In SAIC strategic planning is the process of setting broad goals and objectives for the next three to five years and devising, in general, how company resources should be applied in pursuing them. The aims of this process are to understand ourselves from the viewpoints of both what kind of company we want to be and what real business constraints we face, to be able to assess our successes and failures realistically in these terms, and thus to be better able to direct our human and financial resources toward our long-term goals. Thus, it is essential that managers at all levels become more involved in strategic planning and integrate the longer-term objectives with their own operational plans.

SUMMARY

In summary, the above considerations are set forth to review the current thinking on the kind of company we are trying to build, lest we forget or be enticed into doing something else because of the pressures of the moment. SAIC is a truly unique company—probably the only company of its size that is so thoroughly owned and controlled by its employees and so thoroughly dedicated to national interests. The success we have enjoyed over the last several years has been due to our employee ownership and policy setting philosophy, along with lots of dedication and hard work from everyone in the company. It is vital that the decision process of maintaining sensible, not short-term, goals remain within SAIC. It will take everybody's understanding of what the company is about to continue that process.

Notes

Preface

1. Robert Beyster, "An Emerging and Critical Problem of the Science and Engineering Labor Force," National Science Board, 04–07. See: http://www.nsf.gov/statistics/nsb0407 (January 2004).

Chapter 1

1. Stan Burns, *SAIC: The First Thirty Years* (Del Mar, CA: Tehabi Books, 1999), p. 42.

Chapter 3

1. Posting on Dr. Beyster's blog, www.beyster.com (September 6, 2006).

Chapter 4

1. Stan Burns, *SAIC: The First Thirty Years* (Del Mar, CA: Tehabi Books, 1999), p. 40.

Chapter 5

1. *Expanding Horizons: A History of Science Applications International Corporation* (La Jolla, CA: Unpublished manuscript), p. 40.
2. From Dr. Beyster's blog, www.beyster.com (June 19, 2006).
3. Douglas Kruse and Joseph Blasi, *Employee Ownership, Employee Attitudes, and Firm Performance* (Cambridge, MA: National Bureau for Economic Research, NBER Working Paper No. W5277, September 1995).

4. Richard Freeman, Joseph Blasi, Christopher Mackin, and Douglas Kruse, *Creating a Bigger Pie? The Effects of Employee Ownership, Profit Sharing, and Stock Options on Workplace Performance* (New York: Sponsored by the Russell Sage Foundation, Rockefeller Foundation, and National Bureau of Economic Research, October 6–7, 2006).

5. *Employee Stock Ownership Plans* (Washington, D.C.: U.S. General Accounting Office, October 1987) GAO/PEMD-88-1.

6. Michael Quarrey and Corey Rosen, *Employee Ownership and Corporate Performance* (Oakland, CA: National Center for Employee Ownership, 1986). See also, Corey Rosen and Michael Quarrey, *How Well Is Employee Ownership Doing?* (Boston, MA: *Harvard Business Review, 65,* September-October 1987) pp. 126–130.

7. Tony Vigo, "Employee Owner Relations: Maintaining an Ownership Culture During Change," a presentation at the NCEO 2006 National Conference (April 27, 2006).

8. *Expanding Horizons: A History of Science Applications International Corporation* (La Jolla, CA: Unpublished manuscript), p. 38.

9. From a speech given by Joe Walkush National Center for Employee Ownership Workshop, "SAIC" (Costa Mesa, CA, May 25, 1988).

10. Posting on Dr. Beyster's blog, www.beyster.com (June 9, 2006).

Chapter 6

1. Nola Smith and Peggy Walkush, *1969–1989: SAIC, Twenty Years of Achievement* (La Jolla, CA: SAIC, 1989), p. 4.

2. Dr. Beyster's blog, www.beyster.com (May 21, 2006).

Chapter 7

1. *Expanding Horizons: A History of Science Applications International Corporation* (La Jolla, CA: Unpublished manuscript), p. 26.

2. Stan Burns, *SAIC: The First Thirty Years* (Del Mar, CA: Tehabi Books, 1999), p. 42.

3. See note 1, p. 81.

4. See note 3.

5. See note 1, pp. 31–32.

6. Orit Gadiesh and Charles Ormiston, "Six Rationales to Guide Merger Success," *Strategy and Leadership,* vol. 30, no. 4 (2002), pp. 38–40.

7. Jeffrey Rodengen and Richard Hubbard, *The Legend of the Titan Corporation* (Ft. Lauderdale, FL: Write Stuff, 2002), pp. 18–19.

Chapter 9

1. Posting on Dr. Beyster's blog, www.beyster.com (August 23, 2006).

2. Dennis Conner, *Comeback: My Race for the America's Cup* (New York: St. Martin's Press, 1987), pp. 39–40.

3. See note 2, p. 48.

Chapter 10

1. Posting on Dr. Beyster's blog, www.beyster.com (September 1, 2006).

Chapter 11

1. Harold J. Leavitt and Jean Lipman-Blumen, "Hot Groups: The Rebirth of Individualism," *Ivey Business Journal* (September/October 2000).

2. Jean Lipman-Blumen and Harold J. Leavitt, *Hot Groups: Seeding Them, Feeding Them, and Using Them to Ignite Your Organization* (Oxford: Oxford University Press, 2001), pp. 86–87.

Chapter 13

1. Carl Schramm, *The Entrepreneurial Imperative: How America's Economic Miracle Will Reshape the World (and Change Your Life)* (New York: Collins, 2006), p. 45.

Chapter 14

1. J. R. Beyster, "Employee Ownership: A Key Ingredient for Rejuvenating American Competitiveness," speech to the 16th annual WATTec

Interdisciplinary Technical Conference and Exhibition, Knoxville, TN (February 17, 1989).

2. Al Gore, *An Inconvenient Truth: The Planetary Emergency of Global Warming and What We Can Do about It* (New York: Rodale, 2006), p. 281.

Index

Breinigsville, PA USA
01 August 2010
242572BV00005B/2/P